Hunting Camp 52

Hunting Camp 52

Tales from a North Woods Deer Camp

John Marvin Hanson

WISCONSIN HISTORICAL SOCIETY PRESS

Published by the Wisconsin Historical Society Press
Publishers since 1855

The Wisconsin Historical Society helps people connect to the past
by collecting, preserving, and sharing stories. Founded in 1846, the Society
is one of the nation's finest historical institutions.

wisconsin history.org

Order books by phone toll free: (888) 999-1669
Order books online: shop.wisconsinhistory.org
Join the Wisconsin Historical Society: wisconsinhistory.org/membership

Printed in the United States of America
Cover designed by Andrew Brozyna
Interior typesetting by Biner Design

20 19 18 17 16   1 2 3 4 5

Library of Congress Cataloging-in-Publication Data applied for.

♾ The paper used in this publication meets the minimum requirements of the
American National Standard for Information Sciences—Permanence of Paper
for Printed Library Materials, ANSI Z39.48–1992.

I dedicate this book to my father, to the four other men who called themselves the Jolly Boys, and to the deer camp they called Blue Heaven. This is their story and legacy.

Contents

Preface   xi

Introduction   1

The Jolly Boys   5

Permit for Camp #52   8

Ownership Agreement   10

Construction   12

The Jolly Girls   19

First Shack Log Entry   24

Preparing for the First Season   26

First Deer Season, 1955   31

For More Than Just Hunting   34

Dad's Favorite Place   36

Slow Beginnings, 1956–1957   39

The Long Season, 1958   47

My First Hunt, 1959   49

The Snacks   60

Trails, Roads, and Landmarks   64

Vandalism and Malicious Mischief,
1960–1962   68

Evening Songfests   74

The Light Plant   78

The Monster Buck, 1963   80

Camp No-Hunt, 1964   87

Deer Camps of Like Kind and Quality   92

Deer Camps Remembered   96

The Boot Rack   100

Nightly Card Games   104

The Dog Robber   112

Lost in the Woods, 1965   114

Target Practice, 1966–1967   117

The Coot   120

The Bunny Girls Entertain, 1968   125

Marriage of the Deer Camps,
1969–1970   131

Keeping a Record, the 1970s   137

Three Generations, 1980   140

On the Run, 1981   144

Winds of Change, 1982–1983   147

A New Head Chef, 1984–1986   151

A Successful Season, 1987–1989   160

Butchering the Deer   163

Pratfalls, 1990   168

Adder's Ladder   170

"Snowdin," 1991   172

More Snow, 1992–1993   178

Changing of the Guard   180

Loss, 1994   183

Young Blood, 1995   191

Ghosts and Spooks   194

Our War on Mice   198

Camp Elders, 1996–2000   202

An Uncertain Future, 2001–2003   216

Financing a Hunting Camp   221

Elimination of the Permits,
2004–2005   223

Blue Heaven's Fiftieth Anniversary   227

Final Seasons at Blue Heaven,
2006–2008   230

End of an Era, 2009   232

From Old to New   243

New Blue, 2010–2011   249

Shack Rules   253

Conclusion   257

Acknowledgments   260
About the Author   262

Preface

I have spent all of my fifty-six deer seasons hunting out of the same hunting camp and wouldn't have it any other way. Although I've read numerous books and magazines about white-tailed deer hunting, I've noted that very little is ever mentioned about the activities that go on in hunting camps after the hunt has concluded, and what compels generation after generation to revisit their beloved deer hunting camps each fall.

When the trees start changing colors in the autumn and the leaves begin to fall, I yearn to return to our deer camp. The closer we get to deer season, the more intense those feelings become. I long to smell the familiar aroma of gourmet comfort food cooking in the antique wood stove, and to dine on the time-tested meals that we have served year after year. I am anxious to spend long evenings in the warmth of the camp, sitting around a large table with the people I love, playing cards, exchanging stories, and enjoying the multitude of snacks and beverages that are always available. I look forward to getting away from things most people consider civilized and necessary—no television, no blaring radios, no telephones, and no computers.

You will find some interesting deer hunting stories contained herein, but this is not just another book about hunting white-tailed deer. What these stories demonstrate is that the deer hunt is actually only a small portion of what it means to gather together every fall. To all of us who hunt out of a deer camp or belong to a hunting group, deer hunting is much more than tramping through the woods to shoot a deer. It is about gathering with the same people year after year and strengthening the bonds that develop between fathers and sons, family members, friends, and other hunters with whom one has the privilege of sharing the woods. The memories, the stories that are told time and time again, the camaraderie, the laughter, and the time one is able to spend away from the normal routine of daily life, reacquainting oneself with the joys of nature—I consider all of these things more important than the hunt itself.

Introduction

In the mid-1950s, Sawyer County, along with many other counties in Wisconsin, began to issue Recreational Use Permits on a first-come, first-served basis to people who wanted to construct cabins on county forestland for the purpose of hunting.

These permits were allowed based on Wisconsin State Statute 28.11, which authorized Sawyer County and the other counties in the state to provide recreational opportunities to the public. The statute was vague and, as a result, Sawyer County began issuing permits for hunting cabins at a cost of ten dollars per year, while limiting the number of permits to one hundred.

A permit allowed the permittee to rent county forestland on which to place a hunting cabin. The guidelines for the size of the cabin were dictated by the county, and the cabin was not to be built on a permanent foundation. The permit was conditional and required that the permittee "not cut any green timber, commit waste, or do any damage to the county forest lands." The only privilege given the permittee was to use the cabin for hunting purposes and to cut dead timber for the purpose of providing heat to the cabin. Although the permits were very restrictive, many hunters in the area found them to be ideal for establishing hunting camps in the forest at an affordable cost.

In Hayward, Wisconsin, in 1954, my dad and several of his friends had talked about starting a deer-hunting camp. At that time, memories of World War II were still fresh in people's minds. The members of the "Greatest Generation" were optimistic, though many didn't have anything but their youth and the belief that prosperity could belong to anyone who worked hard in America. That's what my father and his friends believed. My father, Marvin Hanson, married Violet Erickson, whom he met at the Smith Lake Pavilion while performing in the Jack Olson Orchestra in 1939. He entered the navy and returned to his hometown of Hayward after the war ended. At thirty-seven years old, he and my mother, along with my sister Marilynn and me, lived in a house on Fourth Street, which he built under the G.I. Bill.

Sometimes at my dad's grocery store, sometimes on Saturday or Sunday evenings when families would get together and "pass a dish" for a potluck get-together, sometimes in the backyard, but most often while sitting around the kitchen table sipping on a beer, my dad, Merle Dunster, Kenneth Sugrue, Howard Nystrom, and Alvin "Adder" Madson would talk about their dream of building a hunting camp. That dream would become a reality in November 1955 and would become known as Blue Heaven, named after the popular song "My Blue Heaven." Adder loved that song and suggested they call the camp by that name.

The group of men who dreamed it, built it, and hunted from it until the day they died called themselves the Jolly Boys. This book is a recounting, as best as memories and written testimony allow, of the traditions, camaraderie, and love of the hunt that developed in the rustic atmosphere of a Wisconsin deer camp. This is the story of the legacy of one of Hayward's original hunting camps, which lives on, now more than half a century later.

I was ten years old in 1954, and life was a lot less complicated than it is today. My family didn't own a television set. We couldn't afford one, and those who could found very little to watch on their TVs because Hayward was too far from any metropolitan area to get reception. Very little was purchased on credit back then.

The Jolly Boys (left to right): Howard Nystrom, Kenny Sugrue, Alvin "Adder" Madson, Marvin Hanson, and Merle Dunster

Everyone tried to make ends meet with what they had. In Hayward, everyone knew everyone else. Nobody locked their doors at night or when they were away. Most families owned one vehicle, and most were old clunkers, no longer capable of long trips. Very few cars had radios, so when you did go somewhere, you made your own entertainment by singing, which seemed to make the trip shorter. Children spent lots of time outside and entertained themselves with games of make-believe war or cowboys and Indians. We were never bored and neither were our parents. The adults entertained themselves by getting together with friends, relatives, or neighbors. And people always sang at these get-togethers. Everyone worked at least six days a week. Some worked even more. My parents owned a grocery store that stayed open from 7 a.m. until 7 p.m., and sometimes later.

Adults had little leisure time but my parents would put together a party on very short notice. Frequently, one of the neighbors would stop by near suppertime just to say hello and see what we were having for dinner. My mother would invite the neighbor and his or her family to join us, or we would end up at their place for the evening. They would simply combine what was available and put it out on the table for everyone to enjoy. It was a sharing, caring time. When we did end up at someone else's home for dinner, my mother would always be certain that we invited those people back to our house as soon as possible to pay them back. I recall my mother telling my father, "We owe them."

It was against this 1950s background that the Jolly Boys were created. I have enduring and vivid memories of the Jolly Boys' many meetings and conversations as they prepared to begin their project. They referred to these meetings as "going into executive session" and always met in an area where they wouldn't be interrupted and their conversations couldn't be overheard. They weren't interested in anyone else's opinion on how their hunting camp should be operated. Somehow, I always managed to position myself out of sight but within hearing range. They were a diverse group but had one common goal. When presented with the opportunity to lease land from the county, they all knew what they wanted: a hunting camp.

To make their dream a reality, the men needed to decide where to put the camp, how to find the money to construct and equip it, who would be allowed to hunt out of the camp, how they would heat it and provide electricity for lights, how to handle the finances for the supplies, what the rules of conduct and ownership would be, and how to keep the camp alive. Many hunting camps failed and disbanded after being in existence for a short time, and the Jolly Boys were determined their camp would avoid a similar fate.

The Jolly Boys

Alvin "Adder" Madson, the oldest of the Jolly Boys, was in his mid-forties when the camp was first forming. He had worked almost his entire life at Peoples National Bank in Hayward in a variety of positions. He came honestly by his nickname, Adder, which stuck because of his math skills. A strong community and church leader, he was highly respected in Hayward's financial circles. His wife, Ellen, also worked at the bank as a teller. Together they raised three children in Hayward—Sue Ellen, Jay Peter, and Philip—in a white Cape Cod with black shutters across from the Hayward Golf Course. Slight of build but assertive in opinion, Adder maintained an open mind about the world. He was a soft-spoken man who took hunting and the hunting camp very seriously. He possessed a vast knowledge of other hunting camps in the area, and he provided much guidance as the Jolly Boys set about making their hunting camp. He had hunted out of many similar camps and had formulated a strong opinion on how one should be operated.

My father, Marvin "Marv" Hanson, was the son of Bernard Hanson, a well-known merchant who built and operated the Hanson Mercantile Company in Hayward. Marv worked at the store in his youth, acquiring a background in the grocery and butcher business, which gave him the impetus to start his own business, Marv's Super Value, located where Tremblay's Fudge

Shop now sits in downtown Hayward. My mother, Violet, worked
at the grocery store too, ringing up groceries and checking out
customers with whom she was usually on a first-name basis. As
was the practice in those days, driven by practicality and need, my
sister, Marilynn, and I also worked at the store. Marilynn helped
to stock shelves, while I bagged groceries and carried them out
to the customers' cars. My father was respected by the other Jolly
Boys for his cooking skills and his ability to organize supply lists
for what would be needed at camp.

Kenneth "Kenny" Sugrue was the mayor of Hayward at this
time, and he also owned and operated his own gas station next to
the Carnegie Library on Highway 63. He was married to Norma,
whom everyone called Puffin. They had a daughter named Margaret, whom they called Dolly. Kenny didn't hunt or own a deer
rifle, but he badly wanted to be a part of this new hunting camp.
He also didn't drink anything but ginger ale, a trait that no doubt
should have excluded him immediately from the camp. However,
the Jolly Boys liked him and appreciated his mechanical skills,
which were well known in the area and were sorely needed for the
Jeeps that provided the transportation in and out of Blue Heaven.
Although Kenny never hunted, this curly-haired, well-built man
possessed a remarkably sweet, soft, and mellow baritone voice
and could sing with the best of them. The Jolly Boys and their
friends loved to sing, and they were always in awe of the sounds
that came out of Kenny.

Howard Nystrom was a trim and fit man, a Standard Oil distributor for Hayward in those years, who delivered fuel oil and
gasoline to his customers at homes and businesses. He and his
wife, Elva, had two children, Dale and Debbie. The Jolly Boys
always worried about Howard's smoking habit because he frequently fell asleep in his bunk at Blue Heaven with a lit cigarette
still in his hand. Quick-witted, social, and handsome with a per-
petual smile on his face, Howard loved to hunt. But his greatest

fondness for Blue Heaven was in the evening card games and the drinks that were poured as dinner was being prepared on the wood-burning stove. Howard passed away in his late forties of a heart attack, not too many years after the establishment of the camp.

Merle Dunster was the youngest of the Jolly Boys and, without a doubt, the most colorful and charming of the group. He was my father's first cousin and also my father's brother-in-law, married to my mother's sister, Gloria, a glamorous, fun-loving lady known for her beautiful blond hair. They had two children, Barbara and John Kimball, or JK, as he was known, as there were just too many Johns in the family. At the time, Merle worked for Mrs. Sutliff, who owned three lumberyards in Hayward, Stone Lake, and Cable. Merle worked at all three lumberyards, and that connection became critical as the men built the hunting camp. Although he was an excellent carpenter and hunter, Merle's skills were somewhat overshadowed by his antics at Blue Heaven. These included a performance as a Russian dancer one evening, during which a plate full of spaghetti that had been sitting peaceably on the table was kicked into the air, coating everyone at the table in spaghetti sauce. He also spent many evenings wearing Groucho Marx glasses to distract the other card players from concentrating on the game. Merle was always the first to put together an evening of song and performance.

Permit for Camp #52

It was easy for the men to decide they wanted a hunting camp, to name it Blue Heaven, and to call themselves—what else?—the Jolly Boys.

Less easy were decisions regarding location, design, site preparation, legal ownership, building materials, costs, and how the camp would be run. From the beginning, they did not take the decision making lightly. The Jolly Boys knew that underneath the deceptively innocent names of "Jolly Boys" and "Blue Heaven" lay great responsibility that would require fairness, equal labor and input, and consensus on many issues, some of which would not even become clear until the camp was operating.

However, obtaining a permit was the next step to realizing their dream, and for that they needed a location—a tough decision, to be sure, but one my father happily helped to resolve.

I recall that in the early winter deer season of 1954, my dad, along with Merle, Adder, Howard, and several others, went hunting on county forestland about a half mile north of Nelson Lake—an area known as the Totagatic Flowage. This remote area with high rolling hills contained maple, yellow birch, oak, and basswood trees, with many tag alder and cedar swamps, making it an area that most hunters would regard as big buck country. As my father walked on an old, abandoned logging road, he came upon two eight-point bucks running side by side as they came over the crest of a hill parallel to him and heading toward the protection of a large cedar swamp. My father, a skilled hunter with a Winchester Model 94 .30-30, shot both deer. He always referred to those bucks as "twins," and that day he decided that those twins were a sign that this was where the hunting camp should be built. The other Jolly Boys readily agreed, and they assigned Adder the task of getting a permit from the Sawyer County Forestry Department to build the camp in this area. Adder found the precise location in the plat book, and on March 7, 1955, Camp 52 was born.

Ownership Agreement

Protecting the ownership of the hunting camp was of paramount importance to the five original Jolly Boys. They all shared the fear that an "outsider" might create disharmony, which could lead to the demise of the camp. All had witnessed the failure of many other deer camps after resentment developed among camp members. They had heard about camps that had folded when one or more members didn't pay their fair share of camp expenses or share responsibility for tasks such as dishwashing, or cutting and bringing in firewood. They also knew that the younger members needed to handle the "grunt" work, with the older members pitching in to help when possible.

This ownership agreement was simply understood; the Jolly Boys put nothing in writing. If one of the members made the decision to leave the camp, the remaining owners would reimburse the departing member with only his net investment in the venture up to that point in time. The departing member could not sell his share of interest to anyone other than the remaining original Jolly Boys. They also agreed that if one of them should die, the ownership rights would not pass to the man's widow or children. The last thing that any of them wanted was to find themselves in the position of dealing with the wife or children of the former camp owner.

They also agreed that no one would be allowed to invite a guest up to the camp without the prior approval of the others. This was their "blackball" system. They hoped it would prevent any animosity between the Jolly Boys and eliminate the need to cope with a guest that someone else might dislike. Blue Heaven was to be a deer camp where everyone got along, and there was no place for anyone who couldn't hold his liquor or had bad manners. They further agreed that all deer that were taken during the hunt would be shared equally by all. At the end of the deer season, the deer would be butchered, and the meat divided among all who wanted it. The coveted loins and back straps would be reserved for special Jolly Boys parties at the deer camp.

Construction

The Jolly Boys had frequent meetings to plan how their hunting camp would be constructed and equipped. The permit did not allow for a permanent foundation, so they decided to build on concrete block piers. Although the building would be new, they made a conscious decision that they would call their camp "the shack," not "the cabin." Also in the plans, of course, was an outhouse. This would be large enough to contain a small gasoline-operated light plant so that they could have electricity at night, rather than being dependent solely on gas or kerosene lamps. A friend of Merle's donated a 1940s Kohler 1500-watt electric generator, which looked like a small tractor engine. It started with a crank, like an old Model A Ford.

Ultimately, the Jolly Boys chose a footprint about the size of a large garage, measuring sixteen feet wide and twenty-four feet long. They collected building materials from salvaged lumber found in their own garages and backyards, discontinued projects, or sources that might offer it free or at a low cost. Merle, who worked for Mrs. Sutliff in her lumberyards, proved invaluable in obtaining greatly discounted lumber and other materials that needed to be purchased.

They planned for the shack to be oriented due north and south with the entry on the south and the bunks on the north end. Large windows would be installed on the east and west sides of the shack to catch the early morning and late-afternoon sun. The outhouse would be placed about twenty yards to the north of the shack, away from the main entrance for privacy, and the outhouse door would face the east to catch the warmth of the rays from the rising sun.

The Jolly Boys' construction of Blue Heaven began in the summer of 1955, with the intent to hunt out of it by the fall of that year. It was an enormous project. They hauled all of the material in with an old Jeep pickup that Merle owned. Although the new site was only a half mile from a major highway as the crow flies, the old logging road weaving through the woods to the camp was three-quarters of a mile long and frequently muddy, with many deep ruts. The Jeep, as well as many other modes of transportation, got stuck in the mud holes on a regular basis, and it took considerable effort to free the vehicle, which often got stuck down to its rocker panels. There were many work parties that summer. Construction was slow but steady and occasionally complicated by the many mosquitoes, deer flies, and wood ticks that called the forest home.

Merle and Marv square a corner of the shack.

Not many battery-operated power tools were available back then and none were used to construct the shack. Every board in Blue Heaven was cut by hand, every nail was driven by a hand-held hammer, and all of the lumber used consisted of tongue-and-groove planks. Plywood and oriented strand board (OSB) were unavailable or too expensive. The floor of the shack was constructed with tongue-and-groove maple. The Jolly Boys painted it gray because they wanted a floor they could scrub, and scrub they did. They scrubbed their way out of the shack when they left, using a mop, bucket, and Spic and Span, and in the fall of each year, they repainted the floor. Maintaining a clean floor was a cardinal rule of the Jolly Boys, a habit several of them had acquired during their military service. They didn't use insulation in the construction of the shack, so they left the ceiling open into the rafters. Except for the bunk area, which had drywall, the walls were exposed wood, which proved to be the ideal place to hang Playboy centerfolds.

Because the camp permit allowed the taking of down and dead timber for use in the camp, the Jolly Boys decided to use wood as their primary source for heat and cooking, as there was an abundance of yellow birch and maple in the area. One of the most useful finds the Jolly Boys managed to obtain for the shack was an old, black, Monarch wood-burning stove, complete with warming ovens and a warm-water reservoir. It had been sitting, no longer used, in the basement of the old First Lutheran Church where the Jolly Boys were members, and the church was only too happy to trade the stove for the muscle power it took to remove it. Moving that old stove into the shack was an enormous undertaking; it served Blue Heaven well for many years and was the perfect solution for heating and cooking. It served up countless delicious meals and was a constant reminder that "old" was worth keeping and that craftsmanship had value. Next to the stove sat a small, used #1 fuel oil-burning stove, which provided minimal heat after the wood-burning stove had done its job and its fire had died out in the middle of the night.

The men found an old wooden cupboard and placed it inside the shack just to the left of the oil burner and wood cookstove. They used the inside of the cupboard as a pantry to stock the various staples needed to produce meals for the hungry hunters. The top became their bar. Various liquor bottles sat on the Formica surface, neatly arranged and ready for cocktail hour, which began sometimes early, but never later than 5 p.m. Bloody Marys were also mixed there. Everyone joined in for the midmorning Bloody, which was served prior to the huge lumberjack breakfast provided around noon each day, when the hunters came back to warm themselves from the morning hunt. The Jolly Boys drank their Bloodys with a "snit" of beer from the beer keg, which was constantly on tap during deer season. Today that tradition endures, along with a new tradition: Bloody Marys are not consumed until someone has shot a deer and venison is hanging from the deer pole.

In the center of an eight-foot-long kitchen countertop, the Jolly Boys installed an old single-basin porcelain sink. They washed dishes in it, but it was strictly forbidden to use the sink for brushing one's teeth. That had to be done outside. They placed the sink by the main entry, with a window over it so any deer could be spotted while a hunter was on KP (kitchen police or kitchen patrol) duty. Pots and pans were stored on shelves below the countertop. They built three large drawers: one to store silverware and cooking utensils, one for towels, dishcloths, and hot pads, and one for potato and onion storage. There were no cupboard doors; everything was open, neatly stacked, and visible for inspection. The Jolly Boys kept everything in those cupboards sparkling clean.

Central to the shack, the table measured three feet wide and eight feet long, with a matching wood bench on one side and a

number of mismatched chairs on the other side and at the two
ends. It was, of course, a lumberjack-style table, and its functions
included meals, card playing, and cutting up and wrapping venison. On a few occasions it became another bunk when all of the
shack bunks were filled. The table stood adjacent to two large
windows, again to ensure that the hunters could watch for deer
while they sat there.

One of the most important aspects of any serious and respectable hunting camp is the bunk area. In the tradition of the land in
which they lived—lumberjack territory—the Jolly Boys thought
hard about this design. They agreed they needed at least nine
bunks: five for the founders and four for guests. The bunks would
be located at the far end of the shack. Originally, they installed
eight single bunks and one double bunk to accommodate the
possibility of a visit from one of the wives during the off-season.
They later determined that the double bunk wasn't really necessary and took up too much aisle space, so they converted it to a
single bunk.

The Jolly Boys managed to locate used, old-fashioned springs
and single mattresses. They built three bunks against each of the
two walls, and three more bunks between them in the center. The
lower bunks were the coldest at night, whereas the upper bunks
could be quite warm as they were about six feet off the floor. The
middle bunks were coveted, since they were easy to get into and
out of and the temperature was more consistent. Observing the
Jolly Boys select their individual bunks was like reading the story
of "The Three Bears." This one is too high and too warm. This one
is too low and too cold. This middle one will be just right.

My father selected the middle bunk on the left and was always
extremely meticulous when making up his bed. At the beginning of many a deer season, he would haul his mattress out of the
bunk area and put it on the lumberjack table to make it up. He
would carefully put down a sheet to cover the mattress, followed

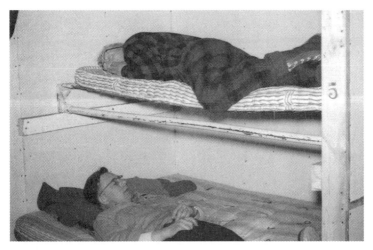

Howard in his lower bunk and Merle in his center bunk take a quick nap before returning to the woods to hunt.

by another sheet. He would then lay two quilts over the top to keep him warm at night. My father always slept in a long night shirt and would often put on a night cap to keep his bald head from getting cold. He always needed help putting his made-up mattress back on his bunk.

Adder selected the center middle bunk for himself, as he felt that sleeping next to one of the outside walls would be too drafty in the early morning hours, when the temperature inside the shack frequently dropped to about forty-five degrees. Adder also slept in a long flannel nightshirt and was equally fussy in the makeup of his bed. He insisted on using flannel sheets, flannel pillowcases, and wool blankets. Merle selected the middle bunk on the right side and was also meticulous about his bedding, using sheets and heavy wool quilts. He slept in long johns, as did Kenny and Howard. Howard slept below Merle and wasn't too fussy about his bedding. Neither was Kenny, who chose the lower center bunk for the ease of getting in and out of it. Each of the Jolly Boys outfitted his bunk area with shelves to keep personal items close at hand. The bunks were sacred territory, and when a Jolly Boy couldn't be in camp, his bunk was to remain untouched. Anyone violating this rule "would be sent packing down the trail," as my father used to say.

The upper bunks were the hardest to climb into and out of, so they were given to the youngest hunters, who would have to crawl up and down using the other bunks as stepladders. The still of the night at the camp was frequently broken by the sounds of men leaving their bunks to go to the outhouse. On occasion, someone would fall out of his bunk and wake the rest of the camp. In what was more an effort to reduce noise from the late-night card playing and storytelling, as opposed to providing a modicum of privacy, the Jolly Boys hung drapes over the two entryways to the bunk area. The drapes also provided a barrier to keep the cigarette and cigar smoke from the sleeping area. And they served another important purpose when someone needed to take a sponge bath during the nine-day deer season. But more on hygiene later.

The Jolly Girls

The Jolly Boys' wives included Violet (my mother), Gloria, Ellen, Elva, and Puffin, and they named themselves the Jolly Girls. High-spirited and good-hearted all of them, these ladies pitched in to assist their husbands in making the shack a success. They went through their kitchens and closets and gave over what must have been, in those days shortly following World War II and not long after the Great Depression, items that meant something to them. They sacrificed pots and pans, tableware, cooking utensils, dishes and glassware, bedding, and towels. Even homemade quilts and coveted flannel sheets were provided by each household. Eventually, many of these items became antiques and collectibles, some rather valuable, but all treasured for the memories and sacrifices they represented.

In many respects, the Jolly Girls came to enjoy the same bond developed by the Jolly Boys. They knew from the beginning that Blue Heaven was for the exclusive use of their husbands, and none of them complained when their husbands left for the nine-day deer season or when it was necessary for them to go up to the shack to handle various construction projects and maintenance. Although the camp was basically an exclusive gathering place for the men in their lives, the Jolly Girls knew there would be many events at Blue Heaven in which they would be included, and all of them were glad for that.

The Jolly Girls (left to right): Ellen Madson, Gloria Dunster, Violet Hanson, Elva Nystrom, and Norma "Puffin" Sugrue

My mother was an excellent seamstress and very talented with her sewing machine. She made the drapes that hung over the entryways to the bunk area. She also made the unique heavy-duty potholders for the cast-iron cookware used on the wood-burning stove. All of the Jolly Girls were superb cooks, and each of them took great pride in sending some of their delicacies up to the hunting shack for the Jolly Boys. One of these delicacies was Ellen's meatballs. She made them with ground beef, pork, and veal, and they were the size of tennis balls. She always prepared them a day or two before the opening of deer season. Adder would bring them to camp, swimming in gravy, to be served on arrival at the shack so the Jolly Boys didn't have to be concerned about preparing the first evening meal. Ellen's meatballs were always served with sliced boiled potatoes and sliced boiled rutabaga with more than ample butter. It was comfort food at its best. When Ellen passed away in 1985, my mother volunteered to take over the chore of making her Norwegian meatballs for us. Although they were good, they were only the size of ping-pong balls. I took over the tradition of the Friday night meatballs when my mother passed away in 2003 and I tweaked her recipe by adding crushed garlic. My two sons who were in their twenties with huge appetites, often competed in a meatball-eating contest at the shack. There was never a clear winner or loser, but both consumed countless meatballs on those first Friday nights in deer camp.

NORWEGIAN MEATBALLS WITH GRAVY

My parents both grew up eating meatballs. My sister and I grew up eating meatballs, and my two sons have inherited the taste and love for what I consider to be the best of the best of all comfort foods. Served with gravy, mashed or boiled potatoes, and rutabagas or a green vegetable, these meatballs will keep everyone at the table until they can consume no more.

My mother's recipe was simple but somewhat bland. She would purchase about two pounds of finely ground chuck and a pound of ground pork and put them in a bowl. She would then add a teaspoon of salt, a quarter teaspoon of pepper, two tablespoons of finely chopped onion, and a few shakes of Lawry's seasoned salt. Next, she would crack an egg and begin to combine the ingredients with her hands. While all of this was going on, she would have a half cup of breadcrumbs or one slice of dried bread soaking in a half cup of milk. After the bread had soaked up all the milk, she would then mix it in with the other ingredients.

Once the ingredients were well blended, the real work would begin. She would start to roll the mixture into meatballs about the size of ping-pong balls and place them in a skillet to fry in a little oil on low heat, turning them frequently so they would brown on all sides. Often, she would sit in a chair near the stove to watch over the progress of the slowly browning meatballs, lovingly turning them so they wouldn't break up. Once the meatballs were browned to her liking, she would remove them from the skillet with a spoon, sprinkle

two tablespoons of flour into the skillet, and shake the skillet
to wet the flour. She would add two cups of cold water and
stir the mixture constantly on low heat with a large fork until
it thickened. The meatballs would then be put back into her
gravy and slowly simmered in the skillet until it was time to
serve dinner with the side dishes that she had carefully selected to complement the meatballs and gravy. Indeed, they
were loved by all who sat at her table.

When I inherited the task of making meatballs and gravy
for the first Friday evening at deer camp, I decided that, although my mother's recipe was time-tested and great, I wanted
to kick the recipe up a few notches and bring it more in line
with the other unforgettable menu items we served at Blue
Heaven. I immediately knew I could accomplish this by inject-
ing minced garlic, horseradish, and additional minced onion
into her recipe. The recipe provides about eight servings.

Ingredients

Meatballs
2 pounds ground beef (80/20)
1 pound ground pork
1 pound ground veal (if veal is not available,
     use half ground beef and half ground pork)
1 cup unseasoned bread crumbs
2 eggs, beaten
1/2 cup milk
1 teaspoon salt
1 teaspoon Lawry's seasoned salt
1 teaspoon ground pepper
1 cup minced onion
1 tablespoon minced garlic
1/2 cup (1 stick) margarine (for frying meatballs)

<u>Gravy</u>
3 1/4 cups milk
Salt and pepper
1 tablespoon horseradish
1/4 cup flour or cornstarch

Preparation

Place all ingredients except for the margarine in a large bowl and mix completely, using hands. Allow mixture to sit for about a half hour. Roll the meatballs in the palms of your hands until they are about the size of golf balls. Melt the margarine in a hot skillet and add the meatballs. Slowly brown the meatballs on all sides until cooked. If you prefer, you can bake the meatballs rather than frying them. Using a shallow roasting pan, bake the meatballs at 325–350 degrees F for about an hour until oven-browned.

Prepare the gravy separately. The best way is right in the skillet using the drippings from frying the meatballs. Remove the meatballs and set them aside in a pan or bowl. Add three cups of the milk to the skillet and turn the heat up to medium. Liberally salt and pepper the gravy to taste and add the horseradish. Using a small shaker or a small glass jar with a lid, mix the flour or cornstarch with 1/4 cup of milk and shake well until blended. This will be used to thicken the gravy. When the gravy begins to simmer, slowly add the flour mixture a little at a time, stirring constantly with a whisk, until the gravy reaches the desired thickness. Turn the heat down and place the meatballs in the gravy, allowing them to simmer gently for at least an hour before serving.

If you've decided to bake the meatballs rather than frying them, I recommend using the recipe for Shack Gravy that you will find with the Shack Steak recipe later in this book. To complement the meatballs even further, I highly recommend placing the jar of horseradish on the table when dinner is served.

First Shack Log Entry

Much of the shack history can be told accurately because the Jolly Boys kept a shack log, a tradition that continues to this day. We now have three logs of recorded stories, told and written by many people who have both known and been a part of Blue Heaven.

The first shack log entry was written by my mother, Violet Hanson. Presumably, it was the first gathering of the Jolly Boys and their families at Blue Heaven. The entry reads:

> Family Housewarming held on Sunday, Nov. 13, 1955—The following people were present: Marvin Hanson, Vi Hanson, Marilynn Hanson, John Hanson, Kenneth Sugrue, Dolly Sugrue, Pete Madson, Merle Dunster, Gloria, wife of Merle, John K. Dunster, Barbara L. Dunster. Boy! Can those Jolly Boys cook! Fabulous meal—pineappled ham, baked potatoes, cole slaw, peas, coffee and cookies. Pony keg too—Lots of fun! Broke camp 5:05 p.m.

The three shack logs are a chronology of all events that have occurred at Blue Heaven from 1955 to present day. The Jolly Boys, their wives, and many of the guests that visited the hunting camp wrote in the log to document memories and impressions of their time spent there, and to preserve those moments for themselves

A family outing at Blue Heaven in 1955 (I am holding an axe in the front row)

and future generations. The camp history within those journals provided the basis for this book and was invaluable to me in my efforts to accurately account the story of the Jolly Boys and their hunting camp.

Preparing for the First Season

As the deer season of November 1955 approached, I watched my father's excitement grow. If we received a little snow, his excitement would escalate, because snow helps hunters to track deer and know where they are moving. Snow also lightens up the woods, making the deer easier to see. Our entire family loved venison, which was what the hunt was all about—the opportunity to bag a deer and provide meat for our table in the coming months.

Dad was going through many of the same preparations as in prior years, but this year it would be different. He now had his own hunting shack; the Jolly Boys had Blue Heaven. My father began accumulating his hunting gear in various parts of the house. His deer rifle had been carefully cleaned and was propped in its case safely in a corner in the bedroom. That way, no one could accidentally bump into it and screw up the sights. He had laid out his box of bullets, along with his deer knife, compass, license, hunting clothes, cigars, and other items "necessary" for the hunt, and he had a checklist for all things critical before leaving for the woods.

My mother took a very active role in this preparatory process. She supported my father's hunting and had taken great pains to ensure that an adequate amount of red cloth had been carefully sewn onto the old wool jacket that he wore while hunting. Blaze orange had not yet become a requirement for deer hunters. My mother, along with the other Jolly Girls, also prepared cookies and other treats to send up to the new hunting shack for the deer season.

My father had a large white duffel bag in which he carefully packed all of his hunting gear. The duffel bag was from his service in the navy, and he used it to transport his hunting gear to deer camp each year until he died. He would pack that bag until it couldn't hold one more thing—and then, somehow, it would hold one more thing.

As an eleven-year-old boy, I wanted nothing more than to go to Blue Heaven with my dad, who was aware of my disappointment that I could not go. I was simply too young to be around all of the high-powered rifles and the "colorful" language that would be spoken by the men while in camp. The Jolly Boys had decided early on that deer season would be for men only, as the shack was too small and crude to accommodate the opposite sex or young children. More to the point, it was their chance to get away from all of the pressures of daily life and to reconnect with nature and each other. They felt that anyone under the age of fourteen was not old enough or mature enough to be included in their hunt while using a high-powered rifle. This was one of their many rules, which all agreed on and respected. It would be allowable for a boy twelve years old or older to come up to camp to hunt with his father for the day, and maybe even stay overnight if there was room, but he would not be allowed out in the woods without supervision. That was too risky for his safety and the safety of the other hunters in the woods. The possibility of young daughters accompanying their fathers to Blue Heaven was never discussed. With the exception of family events, the camp was for men only and that policy remains in effect to this day.

In addition to each hunter preparing his own personal belongings to bring to camp for the hunt, there were other responsibilities assigned to get the camp ready for deer season. My father took charge of preparing the list of supplies that would be needed for the season, Adder made certain that there would be an ample supply of water, and Howard had the job of obtaining #1 fuel oil to operate the oil burner and gasoline to operate the light plant. Merle and Kenny provided the transportation to haul all of the supplies and gear into camp, and they made certain that the Kohler light plant was functional for the season.

The supply list always occupied a considerable amount of my father's time leading up to deer season. He spent hours at his desk with a cigar in his mouth, making certain that adequate provisions would be on hand. The Jolly Boys had met previously in what they termed an "executive session," deciding on the menu for deer camp as well as who planned to be there and on what days people planned to hunt. The list included paper products, pantry staples, produce, dairy products, camp supplies, meat, multiple snack items, and, of course, an extensive list of beverages. Dad began shopping for the supplies weeks in advance, trying to purchase them when they were on sale and then bringing them home and carefully storing them in cardboard boxes to make it easier to transport the supplies into camp. Perishables weren't purchased until a day or two before the big day; my mother wouldn't allow her refrigerator to be held hostage.

Each year my father modified his master supply list, decreasing supplies that he had purchased too much of and increasing the supplies that they had run short of as the season progressed. He had the procedure down almost to a science, and frequently at camp he would quip, if we ran out of crackers, cereal, or other items, "I can never figure out how much you *****s are going to eat up here." It was his standard line every deer season, and he would modify the master list accordingly, trying to be as accurate as possible the following year.

Storing of all of these supplies at deer camp for the entire season was always a challenge. The camp had two discarded refrigerators, which sat out in the attached shanty, to store meat and dairy products. These items had to be closely monitored, as neither refrigerator worked. If the weather was too warm, things would start to spoil, and if the weather was too cold, the eggs and other delicate items could freeze. Often, the delicate items had to be brought in and stored on the shack floor at night to keep them from freezing. At the beginning of the deer season, the cupboard would be overflowing with supplies, and the men always found it difficult to dig through and locate what they needed. Items taking up a great deal of space, such as toilet paper and paper towels, were placed on top of the dish cupboard or in other areas where space was available.

Adder's job of overseeing the water supply was critical. The shack didn't have any running water, as the soil in that area was too rocky for driving a well, in spite of several attempts. Adder would begin filling all the water cans on the morning before the opening of the deer season to get them ready to be transported up to camp. The old milk cans we used had been obtained from Walt West at the Hayward Dairy and were extremely heavy, weighing in excess of one hundred pounds when full. It often took two men to move them. Abundant water was needed for cooking, washing dishes, and having the occasional sponge bath while up at camp. The Jolly Boys heated water in kettles or large pots on top of the wood cookstove. They brought drinking water in empty one-gallon milk jugs, which were much easier to handle than the cans. All of the water was stored out in the attached shanty by the refrigerators. Frequently, the water in the unheated shanty would freeze, so it wasn't unusual to find several water jugs thawing near the cookstove.

The other critical supply item was ice, which was needed to keep the perishables from spoiling if the deer season was warm. The Jolly Boys also needed plenty of ice to chill the beverages and beer for their evening cocktail hours. Everyone who planned on being up at camp shared this responsibility. Each family made several bags of ice cubes or froze water in milk cartons to ensure that there would be an ample supply for the entire deer season. The Jolly Boys never considered spending money to purchase ice.

First Deer Season, 1955

A few days after the official housewarming on November 13, 1955, the shack log records the fact that Kenny, Adder, Marvin, and Merle came up to get the shack ready for the first big day. It had been snowing all day, and the four inches of new snow on the ground obviously generated a considerable amount of excitement in the Jolly Boys.

The shack log entry of November 18, 1955, was recorded by Marvin, who wrote:

> Well here we are!! Got here about six pm. Lots of snow—
> about a foot or more. Howard & Dale, Merle, Marv—Expect
> Pete Madson tonight. Had wieners and kraut, spuds, etc.
> Tapped a "pony." Real good, good, good—This is living. Got
> a dollar apiece on the deer head horns for the first pair of n-ts.
> P.S. No nuts.

The Jolly Boys had established a tradition that each hunter in their camp would place a dollar bill on the horns of an old taxidermied deer head hanging in the bunk area. Merle had donated it after picking it up at a garage sale. The first hunter to shoot a buck during the season would claim the prize money. If no one killed a buck, the money would be placed in the shack fund at the end of the season. In 1955, deer weren't all that plentiful in northern

Marv, Adder, and Kenny proudly display the camp flag in front of the
buck pole.

Wisconsin. Based on data from the Wisconsin Department of
Natural Resources, there were 267,612 hunters and a "one buck,
fork or larger" limit for each hunter, and only 30,000 deer were
harvested.

The Jolly Boys recorded only that one entry in the shack log
that first season. The log has grown in importance and length
every year since then as traditions have evolved and memories
have been created.

In the years that followed, Marvin would often speak about
the difficulties of deer hunting during that period. Naturally, everyone wanted to be up there to hunt, but, due to their work
schedules, it was very difficult for the Jolly Boys to find the time.
Back then, all of them worked at least six days per week and had
very limited or nonexistent paid vacation time. As a result, most

of the Jolly Boys were unable to arrive at deer camp until late on the Friday night before the season opener. The lucky ones were able to get the first weekend of deer hunting off from their jobs or businesses, but the deer camp was usually unoccupied during the workweek. Mostly, the Jolly Boys were able to hunt on the first weekend, Thanksgiving Day, and the last weekend of the nine-day gun deer season. Often, there were too few hunters at camp to have a decent poker game. When only two or three hunters stayed overnight in the shack, they would play cribbage. The beverage of choice back then was beer on tap from a pony keg. The pony kegs of that time were about half the size of the current quarter barrels of beer. They had a cork on the top of the barrel, and the Jolly Boys would compete to see who could shove the tapping rod down through the cork and tighten the tapper before any of the beer escaped. It was a challenge to accomplish that task without spilling a drop, and the Jolly Boys had many friendly arguments as to who was the most proficient.

The meals at deer camp back then were simple fare, as money was tight and frequently there were only a few hunters in camp to be fed. All of this would change as the economic situations of the Jolly Boys improved and their work schedules allowed more of them to be at camp more often.

For More Than Just Hunting

Blue Heaven quickly became a family retreat for activities that went beyond deer hunting. The shack log reflects that on December 11, 1955, several of the Jolly Boys along with their families and other friends went up to the shack to hunt for Christmas trees. All had purchased one-dollar permits from Sawyer County to harvest a Christmas tree that was on county property. It was a Sunday afternoon outing with about a dozen in attendance. A fire in the old wood cookstove warmed the shack, and chili had been brought in for everyone to enjoy. There was beer for the adults and pop for the kids. It was a sunny winter day, with about three feet of snow blanketing the forest floor. Everyone found it difficult to walk through the deep snow, which was almost waist high in places.

Violet wrote in the log, "Merle, Gloria, Barbara, and John walked six miles looking for a Christmas tree and found one scrawny one. These woods are good for other things, but not Christmas trees!" Although many balsam and spruce trees surrounded the new hunting shack, most were either too large to cut down or too deformed to adorn a living room.

Eager to show off the new hunting shack to all of their friends, the Jolly Boys began to invite guests to parties that they hosted during the winter months. The shack log of those early years has numerous entries written by not only the Jolly Boys but also

Violet, Marv, and Ellen pose on their cross-country skis.

many of their various Hayward friends that they welcomed to the shack for these events. Many of these friends became lifelong Blue Heaven aficionados, passing their own stories and memories on to the next generation. Based on the documentation found in the shack logs, one could easily fill this book with stories of all the activities, parties, and outings enjoyed by the Jolly Boys over the years. Let it suffice to say that these events were numerous and always a good time.

Dad's Favorite Place

I don't think anyone enjoyed his time at Blue Heaven more than my father. It was his favorite place to be. He was always in the mood to make the trip up there and could be ready to go at the drop of a hat. He was always willing to put together the supply list to make certain any event would be a success.

He meticulously maintained an inventory of all the staples stored in the cupboard at camp and knew at a glance what supplies were needed. If anyone used any of these supplies without informing him, they would feel my father's wrath when he found the supplies depleted.

God love my mother; she knew how much the hunting camp meant to my father and always encouraged his participation, doing whatever she could to assist him.

My father, like all the Jolly Boys, kept essential personal articles on hand in the small storage lockers assigned to each hunter. Frequently one of the men would be up at camp for a planned day trip and then decide to spend the night. Spare bedding was available to accommodate the unplanned overnight guest, and one might even be able to find a spare unused toothbrush. So many of the events that occurred up there were impromptu, and that was part of the fun of it all.

My parents couldn't afford expensive vacations in faraway places, nor did they have much desire to venture far from home. Their vacation destination of choice was a trip to Blue Heaven for a weekend or the entire week, if they could arrange enough time off work.

Their retreats to the cabin cost them almost nothing, and they took ample food and beverages for their stay. They had this down to a science. My mother would even crack the eggs needed for breakfast and store them in a small mason jar to help keep them cool in their ice chest and as a precaution so they wouldn't break. The same careful planning extended to the snacks they would bring, the ingredients for their meals, and the cocktails and other beverages that would be required. My father always enjoyed a martini or two before his evening dinner, so bringing the right number of olives was also important.

Both Mom and Dad loved to read and would bring a few good books with them in the event that it rained and they couldn't be out in the woods hunting for partridge. My father would sit in his chair at the table, chin in his hands, with elbows planted firmly for support while he read. My mother was more innovative. She would make my father haul up a folding chaise longue on these trips and would position it close to the wood-burning stove to enjoy the warmth while she read and listened to the rain on the roof of the shack. Most days they also managed to sneak in an afternoon nap in the bunk area under one of the many soft quilts. Their cocktail hour would begin promptly at 5 p.m., along with a few snacks, and they often enjoyed a card game or two while dinner was cooking.

My parents learned that it was difficult to sneak away and get much time by themselves. Someone would invariably get wind of the fact that they were going to be at Blue Heaven and would

either pay them a surprise visit or ask beforehand for permission
to be included in the activities. The door was always open, and the
more the merrier! There always seemed to be more than enough
to eat and drink, and those who came up and crashed the party
never showed up empty-handed.

When bedtime came, my father would turn off the light plant
and light the night candle in the event that one of them would
have to get up in the middle of the night. They would crawl into
their bunks, and my father would fall asleep instantly. His snoring
would break the silence and keep my mother awake. To counter
his racket, she would use a small portable radio that had a cord
with an ear-jack for private listening.

My father was dead set against any type of electronics at the
hunting shack. This included telephones, TVs, and radios. He
wanted nothing to disrupt the tranquility of being in the woods.
These and similar items were and always have been banned from
the hunting camp. But my mother needed the device to help her
fall asleep, and, although I think she knew that he knew that she
was hiding her radio, he never said anything about it.

To this day, I bring my mother's radio up to the shack during
deer season so I can get the weather forecast for the day. I will
sit at the table, sipping on my coffee and waiting for the others
to crawl out of their bunks, and get the news and weather from
that beat-up old radio. As soon as the weather is announced, I
turn up the radio and pull out the ear-jack to convert the radio
to speaker so everyone can hear the weather forecast. As soon
as it's concluded, I plug the ear-jack back in so I am the only one
who can hear it. Several hunters in our camp are still amazed that
I can turn on the radio at the precise moment that the weather
forecast is being announced. I am keeping the ear-jack my secret.

Slow Beginnings,
1956–1957

The deer season of 1956 was very similar to the Jolly Boys' first season as the proud owners of a hunting camp. Unfortunately, no deer were harvested. The snow was deep and they found no deer tracks in the immediate area. Based on information from the Wisconsin DNR, that year was still a buck-only season, but for the first time a spike buck was considered to be a legal buck. Although there were 284,645 licensed hunters in the Wisconsin woods that year, only 35,561 bucks were harvested. This did not deter the Jolly Boys. They all loved to be in the woods hunting, and they all also loved being a part of Blue Heaven. If no one shot a deer and they didn't have venison to dine on, they always created an alternate menu for their evening meals. They ate baked ham, beef or pork roasts, or chicken and dumplings. Side dishes included Shack Baked Potatoes and Shack Peas. They kept a pony keg constantly on tap, and they still had their array of evening snacks to go along with the poker games.

A Shack Baked Potato is very much like a potato that has been baked in a campfire. The cookstove's oven temperature is normally about 400 degrees when the firebox is full of wood, and a potato will bake in that temperature in about forty-five minutes. The outside skin of the potato develops a thick, smoky-flavored crust. Served with ample butter, salt, and pepper, it's a treat one does not soon forget. Shack Baked Potatoes can also be duplicated at home in a conventional oven by cooking the potatoes at 425 degrees until the skin is crispy.

Shack Peas are truly a Jolly Boys innovation, served with the majority of the dinners at Blue Heaven, and simple to prepare. They are made by taking three fifteen-ounce cans of LeSueur brand, very young, small, sweet peas and placing them in a pot without draining the juice off the peas. A quarter pound of butter is added, along with liberal salt and pepper, and then the peas are simmered for about an hour on the stove. A ladle is used to dish the peas with their juice into small, individual bowls. One eats Shack Peas with a spoon to get all the fabulous juice with the peas. They make an excellent side dish with a variety of menu items and no one ever dares to refer to them as "green pus bags," the term a friend of mine always used to refer to canned peas.

In 1956 and 1957, the old logging road leading into the camp continued to deteriorate. Vehicles frequently got stuck trying to get in or out of the hunting shack. Transportation was always a problem, and frequently a Jeep stuck in the mud would be abandoned and dug out at a more opportune time. The road traversed several swampy areas, and the soil was mainly rock- and clay-based, making it a challenge to maneuver when wet. The Jolly Boys knew that they would either have to make improvements to the road or find a better mode of transportation to access the shack.

An entry in the log from that season reads: "We left two jeeps mired in the mud at the first bad spot in the turnpike. Ken and Marv abandoned the vehicles and they carried in the water, beer and grub."

Things began to look brighter for the Jolly Boys during the deer season of 1957, as the Wisconsin DNR now allowed hunters to bag one legal buck plus one "party deer" per season. This was the first year that the party deer system was implemented, and

Bob and Howard struggle to remove a Jeep from the muddy logging road.

everyone became very excited over the prospect of being able to get some "camp meat" for the table. To obtain a party deer permit, four hunters had to apply for the permit, and then one of the hunters could shoot a deer of either sex to fill the tag. That year, 288,903 licensed hunters in Wisconsin shot 67,870 deer, almost double the number from the previous year. The Jolly Boys had enough hunters to obtain two party permits. On opening day, Marvin shot a ten-point buck on the same ridge where he had shot the twin bucks in 1954. Later that week, Adder killed a large doe, and his brother-in-law, Norm Schmickel, also filled one of the party tags.

The Jolly Boys were pleased to finally have some venison to eat at camp, but the venison steaks cut from the hind quarters of the deer turned out to be unusually tough and chewy. My father decided that the venison round steaks needed to be tenderized to be edible, and he invented a new Swiss steak recipe for the shack, naming it—what else?—Shack Steak. He cut the steaks into serving size pieces and used a large butcher knife to pound flour into the steaks to tenderize them. He then fried the steaks in Crisco in the cast-iron frypan until they were browned on both sides. Once they were browned, he placed them into a roaster and slow-cooked them in a sauce that he had invented. The new dish was out of this world and is now a regular at our hunting camp.

Everyone left hunting camp that year pleased with the successful deer season. The following spring the Jolly Boys began an effort to improve the logging road leading into the hunting shack. Bob Dunster, Merle's brother, had access to a front-end loader and a dump truck, and he brought them up to see if a bottom could be built in the seemingly bottomless mud holes. The men spent the entire day loading and hauling fill into the swampy areas of the road. Initially, the Jolly Boys thought they were making some headway. However, a very wet summer that year pretty much negated their efforts, and the old logging trail into Blue Heaven remained almost impassable.

SHACK STEAK

Ingredients

Venison steaks cut from the hind quarter of the deer
Flour
Salt and pepper
Crisco or any other brand of vegetable shortening
  for frying
3 (6-ounce) cans Dawn Fresh Mushroom Steak Sauce
  (found either in the ketchup or gravy areas on the
  grocery shelves)
1 (2-ounce) package Lipton onion dry soup mix
2 (13.25-ounce) cans mushroom stems and pieces,
  drained
1 tablespoon horseradish
Water

Preparation

Cut venison round steaks into 3/4-inch serving portions
weighing about 4 ounces. Sprinkle each steak on both sides
with flour. Use a large butcher knife or meat tenderizer to
pound the flour into the steaks on both sides to tenderize the
meat. Salt and pepper the steaks, and place them in a frypan
with an ample amount of Crisco. Fry steaks on both sides
until they are brown and then place the steaks into a roaster.

While the steaks are frying, use a separate pot to blend
the steak sauce, drained mushrooms, and dry soup mix. Add
about 2 cups of water to the mixture along with 1 tablespoon
of horseradish and bring to a simmer.

Pour the sauce over the steaks and add enough water so
that the steaks are covered. Use a tight-fitting lid to cover the

roaster, or cover the roaster with aluminum foil to make a tight seal. Bake the steak and sauce in the oven at 325 to 350 degrees for about three hours. The sauce will initially be quite thin but will thicken during the cooking process from the flour on the steaks. The sauce can be thickened if needed by adding a little more flour or Wondra Quick-Mixing All-Purpose Flour just before serving. The sauce makes excellent gravy for the baked or mashed potatoes that should be served with this dish, and Shack Peas are the perfect accompaniment. The leftover steak makes an excellent hot sandwich. This recipe also works well with beef round steak if venison is not available.

TRADITIONAL VENISON FRY

When cooking with venison, one has to keep in mind that it is a very lean meat and that it is almost impossible to know how tender the venison will be until some of it has been fried and tasted. Numerous factors, such as the age, sex, and diet of the deer, determine whether it will be tender or tough. Venison is also a very healthy meat and, prepared properly, there is nothing tastier. Shack Steak is our preferred method of preparing venison steaks when we find that the meat is on the tough side. However, pan frying the venison is by far our preferred cooking method when we feel it is relatively tender. Because venison is so lean, it is also very dry; there is not much marbleization of fat within the meat, and therefore not much natural moisture to work with. My father always fried venison round steak (steaks cut off of the hindquarter of the deer) and venison sirloins (back straps) until they were thoroughly cooked, taking too much moisture from the meat. As a result, the venison came out on the tough side, even though it had originally been relatively tender. We have learned through the years that the only way to fry venison steaks is medium-rare in order to preserve what little moisture the meat has to offer and to keep the steaks from becoming the consistency of shoe leather. Never overcook venison steaks!

Preparation

Cut the venison steaks into serving portions about 1/2-inch thick and weighing 4 to 6 ounces. The steaks need to be fried in a cast-iron frypan. Cast iron will put a sear on the outside of the meat to lock in the moisture, and using a nonstick frypan will yield unacceptable results. Both the pan and the grease used to fry the steaks have to be hot. The steaks need to be fried quickly on medium-high heat to obtain the desired result.

Place the cast-iron frypan over medium-high heat and allow it to heat for a minute or two. Put an ample amount of either Parkay or butter-flavored Crisco in the pan and allow it to melt. Do not use butter; butter burns. As soon as the Parkay or Crisco becomes sizzling hot, add the room-temperature steaks to the pan. They should immediately start frying. If not, your pan is not hot enough; turn up the heat. Liberally sprinkle the steaks with Lawry's seasoned salt and black pepper. Allow steaks to fry for about two minutes. Watch for blood starting to appear on the top of the steaks and then immediately flip them. Add more Parkay or Crisco if needed and allow the second side of the steaks to fry for another two minutes. Remove the steaks from the pan, serving them while they are still piping hot. (If the kitchen develops a slight blue haze while the steaks are frying, you know that the temperature of your frying pan was perfect!)

THOMPSON VENISON FRY

My youngest son, Ollie, has a very close friend named Danny Thompson. His is a deer-camp family and they have developed a venison steak recipe to die for. Their secret is that they coat the lean venison steaks with flour and seasonings to lock in all the moisture of the meat while it is frying.

Preparation

Place 2 cups of all-purpose flour, about 2 tablespoons of Lawry's seasoned salt, and 1 tablespoon of black pepper in a one-gallon Ziploc bag. Mix contents thoroughly by shaking the bag.

As with the Traditional Venison Fry, cut the venison steaks into serving portions about 1/2-inch thick weighing about 4 to 6 ounces. Place several of the steaks in the plastic bag, shaking the steaks to coat them, and then shaking off any excess coating as they are removed from the bag. For this recipe, it is acceptable to use a nonstick frypan, if desired, as the steaks do not have to sear while they are being fried. They only need to be browned on both sides. Use ample Parkay or Crisco in the frying pan, and fry the steaks on medium to medium-high heat, turning the steaks as soon as blood comes through on the top of the meat. Cook the second side for about two or three minutes until they start to brown and serve immediately. The coating on the meat locks in the moisture of the steak—delicious! We frequently have heated discussions in the evenings when we are about to have a vennie fry regarding whether to have a traditional vennie fry or the Thompson vennie fry!

The Long Season, 1958

On Saturday, November 15, 1958, the first day of the Wisconsin
sixteen-day gun deer season for that year, Merle wrote in the
shack log:

> A large crafty doe, and a lightning fast 8 point buck, at-
> tempted to charge by Merle at 100 yards, but he, also, with a
> lightning fast draw, dropped each with a single bullet. This
> skirmish was at 9:15 a.m. near "The Birch." They were both
> extremely difficult shots thru thick brush with both deer at
> high speed. A medal of merit is certainly due Merle for his
> skill used today.

This was an unusual deer season for the Jolly Boys, because
the state had extended the deer season from nine to sixteen days
in northern Wisconsin. It was also an unusual year for weather,
as the temperature climbed into the high fifties during the day.
There was no snow, and the woods were very noisy. The Jolly
Boys once again had two party tags, and the remaining party tag
was filled with a doe the first Wednesday of the season. The Jolly
Boys decided that a sixteen-day deer hunt was simply too long.
As a result, they hunted for the first nine days of the season and
didn't return to hunt for that final week. For the most part, the
attempt at a sixteen-day season was a bust.

I was fourteen years old that deer season. I remember that although I was allowed to hunt with a rifle, I stuck pretty close to my dad, learning the area around the hunting shack and trying to keep myself from getting lost. I was finally able to experience shack life and to spend a few nights in camp observing the poker games. I was amazed at how much fun my dad and the other Jolly Boys had up there. I quickly came to realize that deer hunting was about much more than the actual deer hunt. The biggest part of the hunt revolved around being in the woods and hunting out of a hunting shack. Getting a deer was almost secondary.

My First Hunt, 1959

I will always look back on deer season 1959 with great fondness. It was the season I shot my first buck. I had spent the previous deer season hunting with my father, who was preparing me to hunt alone safely. I was allowed to carry a rifle, but it was a spare rifle borrowed from one of my uncles. It was different in 1959. That year I was allowed to hunt by myself. I had my own new Winchester Model 94 .30-30, an excellent brush gun known as "the gun that won the West." It was lightweight, accurate, and very dependable. I shot up a box of bullets test-firing my new Model 94, and I spent countless hours loading, unloading, and "dry firing" it in order to become completely familiar with its open iron sights. I believed that I was totally proficient with its operation.

Fortunately, my upbringing involved much time in the woods with my grandfather's Remington bolt-action .22. My grandmother had given it to me after my grandfather died, shortly after my tenth birthday. My friends and I spent much of our free time hunting squirrels, rabbits, and other small game in the woods surrounding Hayward. I considered myself to be a deadly shot with the iron sights of that .22, and I was prepared to move on to bigger game.

That year, I was a freshman at Hayward High School. Like most northern Wisconsin schools, ours was understanding about the nine-day deer season and the tradition allowing students to hunt. School was still in session up to Thanksgiving, but a student was allowed to be absent if he worked ahead in his classes.

I spent many sleepless nights in the weeks before opening weekend lying in bed, thinking about the approaching deer hunt. Visions of trophy bucks danced in my head, as did the gnawing worry that I would miss the buck at which I was shooting or encounter the dreaded "buck fever" that so many hunters spoke about. I had not yet shot a deer. As a matter of fact, I had not yet even *shot at* a deer. The deer herd was scarce in those days, and a hunter felt lucky just to jump a deer or see a "flag" running away from him in the woods.

The time spent in the woods with my father in the seasons leading up to this year had been invaluable. I had learned the essentials of deer hunting and I had learned to do them safely. Hunter safety courses were not required back then; a young hunter learned from the seasoned hunters. More important, my father had taught me about the woods surrounding our hunting camp and the many trails with which I needed to become familiar in order to prevent getting lost in the rugged terrain.

There was an unfortunate complication in the first weekend of that season. My sister Marilynn was scheduled to be married in St. Paul during the late afternoon of the first day of the hunt. My mother gave me and my dad permission to go hunting on opening day, but she said we had to be back home by noon to leave for St. Paul. There could be no excuses for a late departure.

The Friday night before opening day of the season that year was similar to previous years up at the shack. Everyone made their bunks and prepared their hunting gear so that they would be able to be in the woods at first light the next day. Everyone talked about where they planned to be stationed on open morning, and each hunter had his favorite stand where he would be before first light. I was the youngest in the group, and my only plan was to be where no one else was hunting. Adder's wife, Ellen, had made a large pot of meatballs, which simmered on top of the old wood cookstove, along with a pot of boiled potatoes and a pot of rutabagas for our dinner that evening. Several of the hunters gathered at the huge table playing poker, waiting for dinner to be served. I was only fifteen, too young to play poker with the older hunters, so I spent my time checking my hunting gear, making certain that I had all the critical supplies necessary to be carried into the woods on opening morning. I strategically placed spare bullets, hunting knife, compass, matches, toilet paper, candy bars, hunting license, and all the other essentials in my hunting coat, which I kept out in the wood shed so it wouldn't smell of cigar smoke and other hunting camp odors.

Finally, about 10:00 p.m., the poker game ended, dinner was served, and the dishes were washed and put away. Everyone crawled into their bunks to try to get a good night's sleep before the old wind-up alarm clock rang at 4:30 a.m. I crawled into my upper bunk between the soft, old quilts that my mother had sent with me and waited for everyone else to get settled in their bunks so the light plant could be turned off. Merle lit the oil burner to provide heat to the shack once the fire in the woodstove burned out, and he volunteered to go outside and hit the kill switch on the light plant. Once the light plant was shut down, everything went black except for the dim light given off by a plumber's candle that was always lit and placed in the center of the table as a night-light. The only sounds were the hissing of the old large tea kettles on the woodstove, the crackling of the wood burning and snapping within the stove, and the tick-tick-tick of the old alarm clock, which sat in the open cupboards with the dishes.

Although it was only about ten degrees outside, the inside of the shack was warm, cozy, and quiet. Then the snoring began. My father, who slept only about three feet away from me, was the first to drift off into slumber and immediately began to emit sounds that rivaled the noise of an unmuffled chainsaw. Adder quickly joined the serenade. Merle and Howard completed the orchestra with a variety of their own harmonies, and the silence of the camp was gone. I then realized just how hot the upper bunks could get. I had soon thrown all the covers off and covered my ears with two pillows in a feeble attempt to block out the snoring.

The night seemed to last forever, and when the alarm clock rang at 4:30 a.m., I felt as if I hadn't slept at all.

I could smell the aroma of coffee brewing on the gas hot plate that the Jolly Boys had installed for the purpose of making coffee immediately after getting out of bed. The fire in the cookstove had gone out sometime during the night. Getting the stove up to temperature to make coffee would be difficult and would delay the hunters from getting into the woods. I heard someone ask, "What's the temperature outside?" Someone just returning from the outhouse responded: "It's about ten degrees, and the stars are still twinkling, but I can see some light in the east."

I slid further down into my quilts, yearning to sleep until the shack warmed and the coffee was ready. Suddenly, my father shook my bunk violently and said in a loud voice, "Daylight in the swamp!" Reluctantly, I climbed down between the bunks and landed with a thud on the cold floor. The temperature in the shack was only forty-five degrees. I hurriedly slid into my long underwear and put on my wool socks, knowing that it would soon be my turn to visit the cold outhouse. The inside of the shack was full of activity. Merle, the first one up, immediately started the light plant. He now shook the wood coals in the woodstove, trying to make the stove hot enough for the oven to make toast. The other hunters busily got dressed in their hunting clothes and double-checked their hunting gear. Cereal and milk were on the table, and the coffee cups were lined up waiting for the coffee to finish brewing.

Traditionally, the early morning breakfast at our hunting camp is a simple affair. Everyone leaves the camp for the morning hunt and then returns to the shack around 11 a.m. for a large lumberjack breakfast at which stories of the morning hunt are shared and plans for the afternoon hunt developed. There are always several varieties of cereal on the table for the early morning breakfast, the most popular being Raisin Bran prepared with milk and extra sugar to provide needed energy for the hunters. Bread is toasted to a golden brown in the oven, heavily buttered, and served with peanut butter and strawberry jam.

The excitement of the hunt was in the air. All of the Jolly Boys, who had first choice of the prime deer stands, declared where they were going to be at first light. My father said he was walking up to sit near the Little Rocks, which overlooked an extensive area of hardwoods on top of a large hill. Merle was going to his favorite stand, called the Birch. Adder planned to go a couple hundred yards north of the shack to a stand that he called the Chair, and Howard would be hunting the woods just east of the Big Rock. My father told me to walk east on an old logging road that we called Chicago Avenue and head toward the Big Rock area to try to jump a deer or drive a deer to one of the other hunters. The 1959 Wisconsin deer season was designated a one legal buck per hunter season, but as in previous seasons, four hunters could band together with a special permit to shoot a party deer. We had one party deer permit, and the Jolly Boys vowed that the party deer taken must be a large adult deer, not a yearling or smaller deer that wouldn't yield a lot of venison.

Everyone went outside to load their rifles and then headed for their deer stands. They wanted to get settled by the time it was light enough to see down the sights of their rifles. I purposely waited on the road near the shack until I could see to shoot. The eastern sky started to turn pink, and although there were only a couple of inches of snow on the ground, those inches lightened up the woods and made it easier for me to see movement. It was clear and crisp, and the light wind out of the northeast made conditions

ideal for my hunt. My father had taught me to always walk with
the wind in my face when deer hunting. He told me that a deer's
sense of smell is exceptional and that it was a wasted effort to hunt
with the wind at my back. He also taught me to walk slowly and
watch each step, being careful not to step on a stick or anything
else that might alert a deer to my presence. He taught me to be
constantly aware of my surroundings and to look for any object
that might be horizontal to the vertical trees.

By 6:45 a.m. I could hold my rifle up to my shoulder and it was
light enough to align both sights, and I began my first hunt. The
snow on the ground allowed me to move silently down Chicago
Avenue if I walked slowly and carefully. I would pick out a point
on the road, glide slowly to it, and then stand for a few moments,
carefully examining the woods for any sign of movement or ob-
jects that appeared out of place before moving on. I didn't see a
lot of deer tracks in the area, but I did see a few. Whenever I came
across what appeared to be a fresh track, I grew more excited and
alert, hoping that I was getting close to a deer. About halfway
down Chicago Avenue, I was stepping over a windfall on the trail
when a partridge flew up from between my legs. My rifle immediately went to my shoulder, and I had the hammer pulled back
before I realized what had happened. It took several minutes for
my heart to stop racing from the incident.

The sun started to rise, and the woods came alive with activity.
Red squirrels began their noisy chatter, chickadees fluttered between the trees, and crows flew overhead making gurgling sounds
in their throats as they communicated with one another. Every
so often, I could hear the sound of a rifle being discharged in the
distance. None of the shots sounded close enough to be anyone
from our camp, and I wondered if some other hunter had gotten
lucky and bagged his buck. I finally reached the end of Chicago
Avenue at the edge of a large tag alder swamp. Except for my

encounter with the partridge and discovery of a few apparently fresh deer tracks, my hunt thus far hadn't yielded anything.

I was confronted with a decision as to where to go, now that I had finished my hunt down Chicago Avenue. I looked at my watch. It was shortly after 9 a.m., too early to start hunting toward the shack, as I certainly didn't want to be the first one back. I was in a relatively unknown area of the woods, and, although I didn't feel lost, I was somewhat uncertain as to my location. I looked at my compass and decided to walk south, hoping to end up on Birch Street, an old logging road running parallel to Chicago Avenue. I figured the road was about a half mile south of my present location. The wind would be on my left shoulder, and I planned to follow the edge of the tag alder swamp, which showed evidence of established deer trails and a few fresh tracks. The Big Rock was located somewhere in this area between Chicago Avenue and Birch Street. Although I had been there on only one other occasion, I hoped to find it again. I knew Howard was hunting east of there, and I could stand at the Big Rock for an hour or so, hoping Howard would kick a deer in my direction.

Shortly after I left Chicago Avenue to start my hunt toward the Big Rock area, I saw movement on the deer trail coming in my direction. My heart began to race. Was a deer about to appear before me? I quickly stepped off the deer trail, leaned against a large aspen tree, and put my rifle to my shoulder. If this was a deer, I was ready. I then realized that what I had seen was probably too small to be a deer. And that's when I saw what it was. Right in front of me was a huge, fat wolverine walking on the deer trail directly toward me. He looked very mean, as if he owned the woods and I was trespassing. I had never encountered a wolverine in the woods before but was very aware of their reputation for being aggressive and fearless. My mind raced. Do I shoot him or do I yield to him, hoping that he passes by me without an encounter?

I pulled back the hammer of my rifle and decided to give him the opportunity to pass by me. If he decided otherwise, I would be ready for him. He was about six feet away when he veered off the trail and disappeared down into the protection of the tag alder swamp. I released the hammer from its cocked position, both relieved and thankful that the two of us had made the right decision. I was also grateful that I would have an interesting tale to relate to the other hunters when I returned to the shack for breakfast later. It would be my first story for the Jolly Boys.

I continued my trek, walking slowly south on the deer trail. I could see that the trail headed up into the hardwoods above the tag alder swamp. I looked at my watch; it was now almost 9:30 a.m. The sun was fully up and beaming through the trees. The warmth it provided felt good. Suddenly, I heard a muffled noise coming from my left and almost simultaneously saw a deer running perpendicular to me in my direction. The deer looked like a large doe, and I couldn't see any antlers. I quickly pulled back the hammer of my .30-30, put the rifle to my shoulder, took careful aim at the front shoulder of the deer, and pulled the trigger. The rifle discharged but the deer was still running. I quickly ejected the spent shell and fired again. The deer was still running and started to turn away from me, heading up the hill into the hardwoods. Once again, I ejected the spent shell and fired a third shot. I saw the deer tumble to the ground, sliding down into a small indentation on the forest floor. My heart was beating hard and I began to tremble. Had I been successful? Had I just killed my first deer?

I rushed to the area where the deer had fallen and saw it lying on the ground. As I approached it, I could see two twelve-inch spikes on the top of its head. I had just killed my first buck! Hail to the hunter! I was still trembling but managed to pull my deer knife from its shield so I could put my tag on the deer. Suddenly the deer began to move and attempt to get up. Its head twisted back and forth as if it were trying to gore me. I learned an important lesson that day: never approach a deer and assume it's dead until its eyes have glazed over. I quickly grabbed my rifle, which I had leaned against a tree, and shot the deer through the neck at close range. I sat down in the snow, hoping that my hands would stop shaking, and heard Howard's voice yelling at me as he walked in my direction: "Are you the one doing all the shooting?"

"I just got my first buck!" I shouted.

Howard found me, examined the deer, and then shook my hand to congratulate me on my success. He told me that he had jumped the deer in the tag alder swamp just a few minutes before I had started shooting. When I asked Howard where we were, he pointed to the Big Rock embedded in the side of the hill, only about a hundred feet from where the deer had fallen. Howard told me that I had better get busy and "gut out" the deer. Embarrassed, I informed him that I didn't have a clue how to do that. I had read about how to field dress a deer but had never seen it done. Howard took off his coat, took out his knife, and gave me a lesson on the proper way to dress a deer. We had just finished cleaning the buck when Merle appeared. He congratulated me on my success but added that he was sorry he had chosen to sit on the Birch that morning rather than coming to the Big Rock.

Merle retrieved the deer heart and liver from the gut pile, placing them in a plastic bag to be brought back to the shack. They would make pickled venison heart for our snack table and fried venison liver for a future breakfast. The three of us dragged the deer about 150 yards to Birch Street and walked back to the shack. With the Jeep, we would haul the deer back to hang on the buck pole. My father and Adder were already back at the shack, preparing pancakes and pork sausage with fried eggs for our lumberjack breakfast.

My father and I left camp and arrived home by noon to attend my sister's wedding in St. Paul. That entire day, my thoughts and heart were in the woods, reliving the hunt and my success at shooting my first buck. My father and I were back in deer camp by 10:00 that night, ready to hunt again the next morning. Although I wanted to return to the Big Rock to hunt, Merle selected it as his choice for a hunting stand and, because he was a Jolly Boy with the option to do so, I had to find other areas to hunt that season. Two more deer were shot at Blue Heaven that year: another small buck and a party-deer doe. Merle shot both at the Big Rock.

The DNR declared the season a success, as 105,596 deer were harvested by 349,443 licensed hunters in Wisconsin. The Jolly Boys at Blue Heaven harvested three deer with five hunters. We had taken our proportional share.

I shot my first buck at age fifteen. Four years later, I would shoot the biggest buck our hunting camp has ever taken and would also experience what hunters call "buck fever."

PICKLED VENISON HEART

This dish makes an excellent hors d'oeuvre during deer camp, and it's very simple to prepare. You don't often see it served outside of deer season.

Preparation
Take one or more venison hearts and clean any excess fat from the hearts. Soak the hearts in cold salted water for twenty-four hours. Remove the hearts from the water and place them in a pot, covering them with fresh water. Add about three table-spoons of pickling spices to the water, and then simmer the hearts on low heat for about an hour and a half. Remove the hearts and refrigerate them until completely chilled. Slice the hearts thinly and serve on a saltine with a thinly sliced piece of onion and salt and pepper.

FRIED VENISON LIVER

Fried venison liver has always been a favorite for breakfast at our deer camp. Very tasty, but not for the faint of heart.

Preparation

Remove all excess membrane and fat from the venison livers. Place the livers in cold salted water and refrigerate overnight. Remove the livers from the saltwater just prior to preparing, and slice them into 2 to 3 ounce serving portions about ½ inch thick. Place the liver pieces into boiling water for about 1 minute to blanch them. Transfer the blanched pieces to a paper towel to remove excess moisture, then place them in a bag with flour, shaking lightly to coat the pieces with flour. Fry the venison liver pieces in Crisco or margarine in a cast-iron frypan and serve with lots of crisply fried bacon, fried onions, fried potatoes, fried eggs, and plenty of ketchup.

The Snacks

The Jolly Boys quickly earned a reputation for showing their guests how a hunting camp should be operated. It was a ritual that hors d'oeuvres were put out on the kitchen counter for all to enjoy during cocktail hour while dinner was being prepared and the nightly poker game was afoot. After a day of hunting, everyone needed something to tide them over until dinner had been cooked and served later in the evening. The snacks were a meal in themselves. They included sardines; kipper snacks; bulk herring; various types of cheese, "head cheese," and the very smelly Limburger cheese, which was always stored in a glass jar; venison sausage; smoked fish; braunschweiger or liver sausage with a kosher dill slice; and such delicacies as "tiger meat" or, in later years, my wife's pâté. Everything was usually complemented with pieces of sliced onion or sliced rounds of kosher dill pickles and salt and pepper. Tubes of saltine crackers were opened and at the ready to place the snacks on.

The Jolly Boys of old always served "tiger meat" as one of their snacks. This variation of steak tartare was a favorite of just about everyone back in the early years of the hunting camp. My father owned a grocery store, which had a fresh-meat counter. Just before leaving for a trip to Blue Heaven, he would take a few pounds of round steak, remove all excess fat from the edges, and put it through his meat grinder at least twice until it came out the desired consistency. The meat could spoil easily and had to remain highly chilled. He took it up to the shack wrapped in butcher paper. When snack time arrived, he would unwrap the "tiger meat" and put it in a chilled bowl surrounded by ice. The meat would be liberally spread on a saltine with a generous amount of chopped onion laid on top and then heavily salted and peppered. Everyone looked forward to "tiger meat," but it could also generate some lower intestinal distress for those who overindulged in this treat. On occasion, the outhouse behind the shack was fairly busy. As the years passed, this hors d'oeuvre was eventually discontinued.

KATHY'S PÂTÉ

A favorite snack at the shack is my wife Kathy's pâté, which ultimately replaced "tiger meat" at our snack bar. Health concerns arose over the consumption of "tiger meat," and this evolved as a great substitute. We also proudly served this pâté at a supper club that my wife and I operated in Eau Claire, Wisconsin. Kathy was given this recipe in the 1970s by a man named Don Penberthy, an old work colleague in Madison, Wisconsin.

Ingredients
1 (16-ounce) tube chunk braunschweiger
1 (1-ounce) package dry onion soup mix
1 (8-ounce) container sour cream
1 tablespoon Worcestershire sauce
3 dashes Tabasco sauce

Preparation

While allowing the braunschweiger to come to room temperature, combine onion soup mix, sour cream, Worcestershire
sauce, and Tabasco in a mixing bowl. Allow ingredients to sit
for about one-half hour to incorporate. Cut up the braunschweiger into small pieces and add to the mixture. Mix and mash
thoroughly with a fork, or use an electric mixer if available.
Chill and serve with saltine crackers. The flavor of this treat
can really be enhanced by also serving a thin round slice of
kosher dill pickle or onion on top.

THE PROPER WAY TO EAT A SALTINE

We serve only one type of cracker with our multitude of
snacks at our hunting camp: high-quality saltines. They seem
to be the perfect complement to any snack.

One night I folded my poker hand and left the poker table
to fix myself a couple of snacks and mix another drink. I placed
a sardine, a small bit of onion, and a little salt on a saltine. Just
as I was about to devour it, Russ Clagett walked up behind
me. I proudly showed him my creation, which I was about
to consume. I held it up to give him a better view and said,
"Looks pretty good, doesn't it?"

Russ smiled and responded, "Yes, I think I'm also going
to have a sardine, but you have your cracker upside down."

Totally confused by his comment, I said, "Whaddya mean
it's upside down!?"

Russ then proceeded to enlighten me in great detail on
the proper way to eat a saltine. He explained that when the
saltine cracker was baked, salt was placed on the top portion

of the cracker for flavoring. He said it is absolutely essential that when you put the cracker into your mouth, the salted side of the cracker needs to be down. That way, the salted side touches your tongue and you can enjoy the full flavor of the saltine.

I examined my creation. My cracker was indeed upside down; the cracker would not have entered my mouth in the proper manner for me to obtain the full benefit of the salt. I took a new cracker and corrected my mistake. To this day, I have never again allowed a cracker to enter my mouth in the incorrect manner and have since pointed out to a multitude of people that they were attempting to consume a saltine upside down.

Trails, Roads, and Landmarks

After the Jolly Boys had been hunting in the area for about five years, they became familiar with the terrain and knew where they should position themselves to see and kill deer.

I have read numerous books on deer hunting and found that almost every camp has names for the various deer stands, walking trails, and logging roads that run through their hunting area. The Jolly Boys were no different, and they quickly named their deer stands and other landmarks so that when a day's hunt had concluded, each hunter could tell his story of where he had been that day and what he had seen. As I began to become familiar with the general area in which we hunted, I started to make maps when I was about sixteen years old. I transferred that information onto a large window shade along with a separate window shade showing the history of when deer had been shot, the area where each deer was killed, and the name of the successful hunter. I was able to use the shack log to compile this information for the years before I was allowed to hunt up at Blue Heaven.

The area around the shack had a network of logging roads used by loggers back in the 1940s when they were harvesting basswood from the area. The main road into our camp ran from Highway 27 east, past our hunting camp all the way to Nelson Lake, about two miles away. They named this road Birch Street, as it passed by Merle's deer stand, which he called the Birch. Birch

The official record of deer harvested by hunters from Blue Heaven

Street from Highway 27 to our hunting camp was always a mess, because it wound through many low-lying areas with swampland on either side of the road and lots of mud holes. However, after Birch Street passed our camp, the road went into the hardwood hills and became a very decent road with only a few bad spots.

The Birch was in the hardwood hills area, and Merle had built himself a platform among three yellow birch trees that overlooked a vast number of hardwoods, with a tag alder swamp about a hundred yards to the south of his stand. Deer would stick close to the tag alder swamp to escape any danger they might encounter, making this area a hot spot for deer moving through the area. Many deer have been shot from the Birch over the years, and, although the three birch trees are no longer there, the deer stand is still coveted by the hunters from our deer camp.

Just below the Birch and next to the tag alder swamp was a logging road named Snow Plow Road, which also ran east and west, parallel to Birch Street. When the Jolly Boys first started hunting in the area, they found a V-shaped wooden snowplow by the side of the road that had been abandoned by loggers. The old snowplow rotted away long ago, but we still refer to the road as Snow Plow Road.

The Jolly Boys named the other main road in the area Chicago Avenue. This road ran east and west several hundred yards north of Birch Street, terminating at the beginning of a large swamp. Chicago Avenue has several hot deer stands on or near this old logging road. Adder built a platform among three basswood trees, put a chair on it, and nicknamed it the Chair. His stand overlooked a cedar swamp running through a small ravine down to a tag alder swamp. Many deer were taken from or near this great stand, also, which is now only a memory, the platform and Adder's chair having long ago become victims of the elements.

About one hundred yards east of the Chair just off of Chicago Avenue is an area that is called the Ravine, which sits high on a hardwood hill overlooking a tag alder swamp to the north. A cedar swamp next to Chicago Avenue allows for natural deer movement between these two areas. Another hundred yards brings one to a stand called the Crotch, named after a large basswood with a huge crotch in the lower part of its trunk. In this crotch, a hunter could sit to view the surrounding hardwoods and a small creek, which was a natural draw for deer passing through the area.

About fifty yards east of the Crotch is a stand we call the End of Chicago Avenue, which terminates near a tag alder swamp. In recent years, this area has yielded numerous deer for the hunter who has the patience to sit in the early morning hours or at dusk, when the deer are moving.

Branching off Chicago Avenue and running north is a road that has been named North Lane. This road is almost overgrown and has diminished to a faint trail, but it runs through a stand of very thick tag alders and hardwoods that could definitely be considered big buck country.

At a point just before North Lane turns to the east, the Jolly Boys found a five-gallon gas can that loggers left hanging on a tree. They named this stand the Can. Some of the bigger bucks killed in recent years have been shot from tree stands in this area, which is a blend of tag alders, aspens, and pine trees.

Running east from the shack is a road we call Little Rock Road. It winds up a huge hill containing two sizable rocks, which have been inappropriately named the Little Rocks. The view from this stand is amazing. If you continue east on Little Rock Road, you will go through an evergreen swamp and find another large rock called the Big Rock. The Big Rock is actually smaller than the Little Rocks, but nobody has bothered to change the names of these landmarks over the past fifty years. Until recently, due to nearby logging operations, the Big Rock was probably the most successful deer stand in our area.

South of the Big Rock is a stand that we named the Horse Barn after an abandoned one-horse barn used by the loggers years ago. After many decades, the elements have finally rotted the old barn into the leaves. On the west side of the shack, the Upper Swamp Road runs north and terminates in a cedar swamp. It is an excellent hunting area. On the south side of the shack, the Lower Swamp Road goes south down to the Jolly Fisherman Road, which is a main roadway to cabins on Nelson Lake. Logging in recent years has left the area with thick underbrush, and it's very difficult to hunt, due to limited visibility.

If all of these names, terrains, and descriptions leave you befuddled, that's okay. It usually takes several deer seasons hunting these woods before one sees the big picture, but knowing the names of the roads and landmarks is essential in order to relate to everyone else in camp where you have been or where you plan to go during the hunt.

Vandalism and Malicious Mischief, 1960–1962

Sometime during the early spring of 1960, I overheard my father on the phone with Merle talking in a hushed voice. My mother stood close by and I knew something was wrong. I learned that Howard and Elva had separated. All of the Jolly Boys and their wives were devastated over this news. No one knew where Howard was; he had disappeared without contacting any of the other Jolly Boys. Merle and my father decided that they should visit the hunting shack to see if Howard was staying up there. To their relief, they found no sign that he had been there. They later learned that he had moved to the Twin Cities area and that the marriage between Howard and Elva was in the process of being dissolved. It seemed as if there had been a death in the family. They had been a big part of the Blue Heaven family, and this development would leave a noticeable void in the group. We never saw Howard again. Several years later, we found out that he had remarried and had then passed away a few years later from a heart attack.

Although the Jolly Boys made occasional inspection trips into the shack over the summer, they seldom used the shack for recreational activities at that time of year as it was too difficult to cope with the wood ticks, mosquitoes, and deer flies. The grass around the shack grew waist high during the summer months and had to be cut down in the fall when the weather cooled and the growing season ended.

All of the Jolly Boys and their families looked forward to the first weekend in October. By that time of year, the weather was cool enough to build a fire in the wood-burning stove, the bugs had pretty much disappeared, and the fall colors were in their full glory. Both my mother and Merle's daughter, Barbara, were born on October first, and everyone looked forward to going to the shack to celebrate the birthdays. We also used the occasion to open up and clean the shack for the upcoming hunting season. The men would bring their shotguns and walk the many roads and trails in the area, hunting for partridge and checking out recent signs of deer for the upcoming season. Many would choose to stay overnight.

The standard Saturday evening dinner consisted of a huge beef pot roast with carrots, onions, and potatoes, or a large pork roast with summer squash and mashed potatoes. Of course, we always made plenty of delicious gravy. My mother referred to the areas around the shack at this time of the year as "the golden land." I too use that term with my wife, Kathy, when we drive through all of the woods and trails that I favor in the fall. There is nothing more beautiful than maple trees in their full golden color against a deep blue sky. Even today the roads are marked as the "Fall Color Tour." I can still hear my mother singing, "Autumn leaves are now falling, see them tumbling down. . . . Autumn leaves are now falling, red, yellow, and brown."

The Jolly Boys did not write much in the shack log about the 1960 deer season. It reflects the fact that I shot two does at the Big Rock and that Philip "Flipper" Madson, Adder's youngest son, shot a five-point buck in the balsam pines just south of Birch Street. Flipper was about fourteen at that time and hunting close to his father when he saw a deer running at full speed and managed to shoot it after several shots. I had been hunting near an area we call Bullshot Corner, about a hundred yards west. I heard several shots and knew that Adder and Flipper were hunting in that area. I decided to head in that direction to see if they needed any help.

~~It was a beautiful day with mild winter temperatures and knee-~~ high snow on the ground. It was slow going, but as I got closer to the area where I had heard all the shooting, I could see three hunters standing together, apparently arguing. As I got closer, I recognized Adder and Flipper but did not recognize the other hunter, who had his back toward me. As I approached, I could hear the stranger loudly arguing that Flipper had shot the stranger's deer, which he claimed to have shot and wounded minutes before the deer came up on Flipper. Flipper wasn't saying much but Adder argued that the deer might have been slightly wounded but was running through the woods at express-train speed when shot by Flipper. They were at a stalemate as to who had the right to the deer, neither willing to concede the kill.

The woods were so quiet with all the snow that the stranger had not heard me approach from behind, though Adder and Flipper had seen me coming. Eventually, the stranger must have felt my presence about twenty feet behind him. He suddenly turned and looked startled to see me standing there with my .30-30 cradled in my arms, my hand in the lever and my finger on the trigger. The stranger must have realized that this was an argument he wasn't going to win with the three of us surrounding him. He was upset but walked away. I watched him closely until he disappeared from our view. It was my first and only confrontation with a hunter over who had the right to a wounded deer. I hoped that it would never happen again. I became aware that day that every hunter wants to claim his deer. It was an instinct that I had learned from my father and one that goes to the heart of not just the kill but the pride of the hunt.

The following deer season, 1961, was pretty much a loss for the hunters at Blue Heaven. The weather was too warm, there was no snow, and the woods were very dry and noisy. We all suspected that most of the deer had left our area in an attempt to find water, as even the swamps were dried out. My father and I, along with Merle and his navy friend Bob Larson, Adder and his two sons, and Merle's son JK, spent the entire season hunting without seeing any deer. On the last Saturday of the nine-day season, Kenny invited his new son-in-law, Harry Lippert, to the shack to hunt with us and see what our hunting camp looked like. Harry had never been in the area before, but walking north of the shack near the section we call the Can, he came across an old, gray ten-point buck and downed the deer with one bullet. He dragged the deer back to the shack by himself. As we all inspected his trophy, we witnessed dozens of wood ticks crawling off of it. It was unusual to see all of these insects abandoning their host, and we wondered why this deer had so many wood ticks attached to it. We never did figure it out. That evening, Harry took his deer, wood ticks and all, back home to skin it out and cut it up, since the weather was too warm to allow it to hang for very long.

The following summer, Merle made an inspection trip into the shack and found that a porcupine had eaten through the wire mesh on our vent window and entered the shack. He killed it with a pitch fork that was available in the shanty. Porkies, as we call them, love salt and will chew on anything and everything that has been touched by the human hand. This porky had done considerable damage, having chewed on the backs of all the chairs, the entry door, and many other things in the shack. The porky had taken up residence for quite some time and filled the place with its droppings. The shack was a mess, and the following weekend, everyone came up to witness the damage and clean things up.

In those days, porkies were plentiful in the area and could be seen high in the tops of basswood trees. In the fall of 1960, a porcupine had forced its way into the outhouse and chewed the heck out of the wood interior. They were starting to become a problem for us. From that point forth, we declared war on porcupines in

the area and issued an order to kill any seen within a mile of the
shack. This went against the Jolly Boys' philosophy, because we
all believed that nothing should be killed unless the meat would
be consumed. It was also common knowledge that a porky was a
very slow animal and a hunter could actually catch one by hand
and use it as a food source if he became lost in the woods. Nonetheless, after the onslaught, if a porky was seen near the shack, it
was eliminated.

Porcupines were not the only destructive problem that the
Jolly Boys had to address that year. They had always considered
themselves fortunate that the shack had escaped any vandalism or
theft. It was far from the nearest highway and the road leading into
the shack was almost impassable. Therefore, it was very unusual
to see anyone coming back into that area, unless it was someone
we knew and who knew the shack's location.

Over the years, I had invited several of my friends up to the
shack to hunt partridge or squirrels, and many of them knew the
location of the shack and the hidden door key. One fall evening,
unbeknownst to me or anyone else, a group of my seventeen-
year-old friends made a trip into the shack with several cases of
beer. They intended to use the shack to party and drink, and to
leave it undisturbed. They let themselves in using the key to the
door and spent several hours drinking beer. They all became quite
intoxicated, and someone accidentally broke a dish or a glass on
the floor. The other boys quickly joined in on the carnage. By the
time they were done, they had broken all of the dishes, all of the
windows, and anything else that could be shattered.

Merle made a routine inspection trip to the shack the following day and discovered the vandalism. He immediately contacted
the sheriff, and a deputy was dispatched to document the damage
and investigate the incident. While Merle and the deputy were
still there, one of my friends, whose guilt had gotten the better of
him, returned to the scene of the crime to inspect what they had

done the night before. Merle and the deputy immediately knew that this individual had been involved, and after a short period of questioning, he confessed and named his accomplices. The parents of my four friends were contacted, and all came to the shack to clean up the mess, repair the damage, and offer restitution for the items that couldn't be repaired. The Jolly Boys had a meeting and decided not to file charges, as they believed that the parents would be able to impose suitable punishment. As a result, my four friends involved in the incident were all kicked off the football team, and most of their parents grounded them for the rest of their natural lives. To this day, it is a regrettable memory but one that enforces the sanctity of the camp: Thou shalt honor it.

Evening Songfests

I find it difficult to describe how much the Jolly Boys and their friends loved singing at Blue Heaven. The singing sessions would begin when the poker game had concluded and when the evening meal was on the table.

The lengthy happy hours leading up to the songfest played no minor role in putting everyone in the mood to sing. Merle usually initiated the shack sing-a-long by jumping up from the poker game and passing out songbooks to everyone. The songs they sang were primarily from the 1940s—songs well known to all of them, rooted in memories of the World War II era. Classic hits like "Goodnight, Irene," "Paper Doll," "Only You," "Peg O' My Heart," "You Made Me Love You," "It Had to Be You," "I'm Looking Over a Four-Leaf Clover," "I'll Get By," and "If I Loved You" were just some of the standards. Of course, the Jolly Boys' favorite song was "My Blue Heaven."

One of the Jolly Boys had "mimeographed" the lyrics of many popular songs and put them into booklet form so everyone could sing along without missing a word. All of the shack residents knew the melodies, and no one had a problem with volume.

Some of the songs, by groups such as the Mills Brothers and the Platters, begged for harmony. Valiant attempts were made, but harmony was not always achieved.

Marv and Merle lead everyone in song.

My father was an experienced bass from years of playing bass instruments in a dance band, and he also had practical experience singing bass in the church choir. Kenny Sugrue had a mellow voice that was admired by all, and a special gift of soft vibrato in his voice. He would usually take the lead in starting each song in the proper pitch. Merle would always sing the lead part and did so with a great deal of volume and enthusiasm. Frequently, the veins in his forehead and throat would stand out as he attempted to drown out the others in the group. The other participants would either follow my father in the bass part or sing lead along with Kenny. On the rare occasion when everyone actually produced a decent-sounding chord, the group would stop and revisit that part of the song. They sometimes surprised themselves.

Radios and mechanical devices for the reproduction of music at our hunting camp were forbidden. We always made our own music and entertainment, a practice that has carried on to this day. The songfest tradition carried over into all the gatherings at

Merle plays the tonette during a nightly sing-a-long.

the hunting shack. Whenever people visited the shack, there was music. After my father passed away in 1994, much of that music at Blue Heaven died with him. The generation that followed wasn't familiar with the songs in the song books. But late at night when the lights are out and the bunks are full, I can almost hear the Jolly Boys and all their friends still singing the old songs.

The Light Plant

In the fall of 1963, the Jolly Boys decided that it was time to replace the Kohler light plant that Merle's friend Adrian Faase had donated to Blue Heaven. The light plant was a four-cylinder, four-stroke, gas-operated engine with a two-inch bore and a three-inch stroke. It generated 1,500 watts of DC power at 115 volts and operated at 1,000 rpm. The putt-putt-putt sound that it generated was a soothing background effect, comforting to all who spent any time up at the hunting shack.

The light plant was the ideal solution to generate electricity for the shack, but the Jolly Boys had grown impatient with its mechanical problems. Many times the light plant wouldn't start, and several times it had quit operating and couldn't be restarted. The light plant had been operating in the same small building that served as our outhouse, and although it provided some heat for the hunters while they used the outhouse, the men found it too difficult to work on in such a small space.

Merle, Adder, Adder's oldest son, Peter, and I drove to the shack early in September of that year and poured a concrete slab for the replacement. On top of the slab, we poured a concrete stand to bolt down the engine. We found an old outhouse that was still in good condition and attached this building to the slab. It was hard work mixing all of the concrete by hand in a wheelbarrow, but things went smoothly. A couple of weeks later, we

The Kohler light plant, our dependable source of electrical power for
Blue Heaven

returned to install the replacement light plant, which was identical to the original. We saved the old light plant for spare parts,
as that model had been discontinued by the manufacturer and
replacement parts were very difficult to obtain. Late that evening,
we lifted the new, five-hundred-pound light plant onto its concrete pedestal, getting it installed and operating. It purred like a
kitten, and the lights were 100 percent brighter. The project was
declared a success.

Over the years, we have purchased two similar light plants
strictly for the purpose of supplying spare parts to keep the current light plant functional. The old Kohler light plant remains our
main source of electrical power to this day.

The Monster Buck, 1963

There are only four short entries in the shack log from the 1963 deer season, one of which includes a major historical event.

> 11/22/63—Marv & Bob H. came out in PM with supplies.
> Merle at about 8. John H. and Flipper after BB game.
> Pres. J. F. Kennedy assassinated.
> 11/23/63—John H. got his buck—12 (?) pointer.
> 11/25/63—John K. Dunster got 1st shot at buck. Merle,
> John H., and John K. tracked for 4 hours & came out near
> Seeley fire lane. Didn't find.
> 11/26/63—Ken S. out for delicious ribs & kraut. Delightful
> poker game.

Although the shack log didn't record much detail of that deer season, I still recall all of the events of that week.

I was nineteen and had taken a semester off from college to take a job at a woodworking factory in Hayward. I needed to earn tuition money so I could return to school for the second semester. On Friday, November 22, 1963, I was packed and eagerly awaiting the factory's closing whistle at 3:30 that afternoon. Shortly after our lunch break, I saw one of my coworkers racing between the different employees in our area of the factory and yelling something, but I couldn't hear him over the dozens of saws that were in operation. Finally, he arrived at my workstation. His face was pale, and he yelled in my ear, "President Kennedy was shot and killed in Dallas this afternoon!" Several of my coworkers had already shut their machines off and were heading to the parking lot to listen to their car radios for more information. I did the same. Available information was limited, but it soon became evident that President Kennedy had been assassinated and that the assassin had been captured right after the incident. I had the same thoughts as everyone else: Was it connected with the Russians? Were we going to war? Under the circumstances, would we have deer season this year or should we cancel it and remain home close to our families?

The plant manager gathered everyone together and told us that we could all go home early that afternoon. I used one of the office phones and called my father. He had heard the news and was very upset. However, he sounded relatively calm and assured me that we would still be heading to deer camp. We would take portable radios up with us to keep in touch with the outside world and would return home if necessary. The excitement of the impending hunt was greatly overshadowed by the uncertainties of that day's events. Our usual Friday night prehunt excitement was replaced by a somber atmosphere, and we spent the majority of that evening listening to the radio for any new developments regarding the future of our country. When we crawled into our bunks that evening, we were all thinking more about the day's events than about the opening day of deer season, which was only a few hours away.

The shack alarm clock sounded at 5:00 the next morning. We immediately turned our portable radio on for any news and were relieved to learn that the assassination was apparently the work of one lunatic and we weren't going to war with the Russians or anyone else. The vice president had been sworn in as our new president, and it seemed that the FBI had everything under control.

We could now concentrate on the hunt without worrying about having to return home.

In addition to my dad and me, our hunting group that year included my dad's younger brother Bobby, Adder and his two sons, Peter and Philip, along with Merle. As a group of seven, we would have decent hunter saturation in the woods on opening morning, and we were all optimistic that one of us would shoot and kill a deer. Everyone announced where they planned to sit on that first morning, except me. I wasn't much good at "sitting." I planned to slowly hunt while walking east on Chicago Avenue until I reached the Crotch. I would stand there for a bit and then move on when I tired of looking at the same piece of woods. I was too impatient to stand or sit in one location for too long—I always had to see what was going on over the next hill. I had developed my own style of hunting. I loaded my Winchester Model 94 .30-30 with eight bullets. I inserted seven in the tube of the rifle and locked one in the chamber. I left the warmth of the hunting shack at 6:30 that morning, ready for action, just as it was getting light enough to see the front and rear sights of my rifle.

I walked about fifty yards through the woods, arrived on Chicago Avenue, and began my hunt. There was only a trace of snow on the ground, so even walking was noisy, with the still-frozen leaves covering the road. I took every step slowly and carefully, trying not to step on a branch or give any indication that I was moving through the woods. I would move slowly for about twenty-five or thirty yards, and then stop for a minute or two to look and listen to see if there was any movement in the woods ahead of me, on my sides, or to my rear. My father had taught me well in this regard, pointing out that trees grow vertically, and that I needed to look for anything that was horizontal or looked out of place. I also looked for any disturbance of the ground covering, which might indicate that there were deer in the area. The skies were clear, so the woods were getting brighter by the minute and the sun would soon be filtering through the trees. The sun would be warm enough to melt the little bit of snow on the ground, so it would be a difficult day for anyone to track a wounded deer.

I continued my hunting method, traveling east on Chicago Avenue for about half an hour. Slow walk. . . . Stop. . . . Look. . . . Listen. . . . Eventually, I reached a point where the Crotch was almost in view. I noticed a few deer tracks in the area, but none appeared to be fresh. I could hear frequent shots being fired nearby, but not close enough to be anyone from our hunting party. To my left was an evergreen swamp with a heavily mossed floor and a combination of cedar and hemlock trees. It was a beautiful area, and I had walked through it many times in past deer seasons, always finding numerous deer beds. The trees were mature, and one could look through the swamp to higher ground beyond. The swamp was alive with early morning activity. Chickadees fluttered between the trees. Red squirrels ran around underneath the trees, chasing each other and giving their shrill warning cries to let everyone know that a stranger was approaching the area. All of a sudden, I saw a flash of movement. My rifle went immediately to my shoulder, but by the time I pulled my hammer back, I realized it was only a partridge. I had spooked it, and it was flying away from me to make its escape. I lowered my rifle, released the hammer, and continued my slow walk past the swamp. The Crotch came into my view, and the snow on the ground showed that there had been considerable deer activity in that area overnight. I was starting to feel very optimistic that I might see a deer.

I'm not certain to this day whether I heard the deer and then saw it, or saw the deer and then heard it. About seventy or eighty yards to my right, a huge deer came running perpendicular to me at almost full speed down the hill through the basswoods. Obviously, it had been kicked out by another hunter, and the deer was heading to the tag alder swamp just to the north of the Crotch, seeking safety. I instinctively pulled the hammer back on my .30-30 and raised the rifle to my shoulder, took careful aim at the animal's left front shoulder, and fired.

The bark from my rifle broke the tranquil silence of the swamp, and all of the animals within went on full alert. I quickly ejected the spent shell, aimed, saw the magnificent antlers on the deer shining in the morning sun, and fired again. I ejected and fired five more times, and on my eighth shot, I saw the deer stumble and crash to the forest floor. My heart was racing and my hands were trembling. My rifle was empty. I threw off my gloves and fumbled through my jacket pocket. I pulled out five more bullets and shoved them into my .30-30.

The deer was down but still making a valiant attempt to get back up and run to safety. He could raise his hind legs but was unable to raise himself up on his front legs. I fired again, and again, and again, and again. He finally stayed down and I ran over to where he lay. The magnificent animal was taking his final breaths. I raised my rifle and fired my remaining bullet into his thick neck. There was no further movement. I sat down on a windfall near him, marveling at him. My hands were still trembling, but I managed to reload my rifle with a few additional bullets just in case he miraculously recovered and attempted to escape. The green swamp, now to the back of me, quickly quieted down and returned to its peaceful and tranquil state.

After a few moments, I collected myself, stood up, leaned my rifle against a nearby tree, and grabbed the buck by its antlers. I thought I had shot a ten-point buck, but there were twelve large points with two smaller points on each side of the rack. It was a legal sixteen-point buck! His coat was gray, and his teeth were worn down, indicating that he was an old, wise, swamp buck that had escaped death and eluded hunters' rifles over the course of numerous deer seasons. He was a trophy, and he was my trophy.

I took off my jacket and field dressed him. I wiped my hands on several red handkerchiefs that I had with me, left the deer in the woods, and began the forced march back to the shack. On my arrival, the shack was empty and it was only about a quarter after eight. I walked over to the old deer head with the buck dollars on it, removed them, and put them in my pocket. I didn't want to risk having my trophy discovered in the woods by another hunter, so I started the Coot and drove back to the scene of the kill. On my way, I picked up Peter, and the two of us loaded the deer into the back of the Coot. The deer was heavy, and it was all that the two of us could do to lift him and load him into the back. We transported the deer back to the shack, and it took four of us to lift him up and secure him on the buck pole. My father returned for breakfast, admired my kill, and examined the carcass of the deer. He came to the conclusion that I had hit the deer a total of five times. In addition to the bullet in the deer's neck, one bullet had broken the deer's left front foreleg, a bullet had hit and broken the deer's spine just behind the front shoulders, and the other two bullets had landed solidly in the chest. There were no other wounds.

Later that evening, I related the tale of the hunt to the other hunters sitting around the table. Although I insisted that I had fired all eight bullets in my rifle and then reloaded and fired an additional five rounds, everyone insisted that they had only heard five shots, not thirteen. The next morning, Peter walked back and located the spot in the road where I had been standing when shooting at the deer. He kicked around in the leaves and was able to find all thirteen of my shells. He brought them back to the shack with him when we all gathered for our late morning breakfast. He once again asked me, "How many times did you say you shot at that buck yesterday?" I responded, "Thirteen." He then gave me one of the biggest grins I've ever seen in my life and pulled the thirteen shells out of his pocket, laying them on the table. Five of the bullets were spent. The other eight bullets were still fully loaded. I sat there quietly and stared at the bullets. I had experienced "buck fever" and had been totally oblivious to the fact that I had only fired five bullets. The other bullets had been ejected from my rifle without being fired. I had been so excited that I was double- or triple-cocking my .30-30 as I shot at the deer.

We brought the deer into town at the end of deer season and stopped by the local feed mill to have it weighed. It dressed out at 232 pounds, and the antlers were twenty-four inches wide. A true trophy. I cut the antlers off the head, mounted them on a wooden plaque, and returned them to the shack in the spring. I nailed them above the entry for everyone to hang their hats on for good luck. Unfortunately, a porcupine slid down the chimney connected to our cookstove that summer. It entered the shack through the stove and chewed on everything it could sink its teeth into. Porkies love deer antlers, and my trophy rack is now only a memory.

Camp No-Hunt, 1964

Deer season 1964 was unusually cold, with subzero temperatures and very little snow cover. I shot a small buck at the Big Rock early opening afternoon, but the other hunters didn't see any deer on that opening weekend.

We were developing a tradition that on the first Sunday evening of the deer season, Camp No-Hunt would come to Blue Heaven to celebrate or we would go over to their camp to be entertained.

Camp No-Hunt was also known as Hunters, Inc., and the members of their camp had also taken advantage of the Recreational Use Permits that were offered in the mid-1950s. The seven members of the camp were all prominent Hayward businessmen and were slightly older than the Jolly Boys. They built their own camp on Bayfield County forestlands about ten miles west of our shack. I don't know this to be true, but rumor had it that the members of their camp were forbidden to shoot any deer, and any member violating that rule would be banned from their hunting camp. I never remember any deer hanging from their buck pole, and I never saw any sign that a deer had been hanging there.

Camp No-Hunt was a fun-loving, mischievous group of men, and the biggest rascal of the bunch was Orville "Dane" Nelson. In addition to his skills as a carpenter, Dane also served as the first sergeant of the local National Guard unit, which was a combat

Members of Camp No-Hunt (also known as Fort Nelson) greet the Jolly Boys with song.

engineer battalion. Dane had extensive knowledge of and access to a multitude of devices with trip wires, many with the capacity to generate loud, explosive warnings that the enemy was approaching. One could never approach their camp unannounced, as Dane had affixed warning devices on the roadway to their camp, the areas surrounding it, and even the outhouse door. He was the self-appointed sergeant-at-arms for Camp No-Hunt and took his position very seriously. He never showed up at our camp without wearing his first sergeant shirt and combat engineer beanie, and he never failed to make us roll with laughter.

One Sunday evening in November 1964, the seven members of Camp No-Hunt arrived at Blue Heaven promptly at 5 p.m. They had all crammed into Harold Gobler's four-door Jeep Wagoneer, and they were ready to party. As usual, the road to our shack was in horrible condition. Although the temperature was well below zero, the large mud hole just below our shack had not completely frozen over because of the constant traffic it had seen on the opening weekend of deer season. Harold's Jeep was a muddy mess after crashing through the final mud hole to reach our shack.

The shack log from November 22 recorded this:

Big party at Bloo Heaven. Guests included the members of Camp No-Hunt, Fr. Bob Hanson, Bob Hanson, Vern Inhoff, Don Gillis and Curt Karbalis. Carl Bensen bled a little. Dane felt pretty bad. Wonderful party!

As was the custom, everyone enjoyed a long happy hour, complete with lots of snacks, and then joined in a songfest until dinner was served. The menu included prime rib, crisp-skinned baked potatoes from the woodstove, Shack Peas, and salad. There were about seventeen for dinner that evening, so the Jolly Boys had to serve dinner in shifts. When dinner had concluded, everyone said their goodbyes, and the members of Camp No-Hunt all piled

Adder, Bob Hanson, Marv, Vern Inhoff, and Kenny dine on a meal served by members of Camp No-Hunt.

into Harold's Jeep for the trip back to their shack. It was bitterly cold outside by that time. Harold put the vehicle in gear, but it wouldn't move; all four wheels were completely frozen from the water in the mud hole on the trip in.

Everyone pitched in to try to get the vehicle to move, but it wouldn't budge. Kenny even started up his Jeep to give Harold's vehicle a push, hoping that would free the wheels. Nothing worked. Finally, Harold became impatient, threw the vehicle in gear, and pressed the accelerator to the floor. Horrible odors came from that old Jeep as the transmission blew and the engine fried. The vehicle was toast. Since Blue Heaven could only accommodate nine hunters comfortably overnight, the Jolly Boys had to transport the Camp No-Hunt members back to their shack. Harold's Jeep sat next to our shack for the rest of the deer season and was not returned to town until the road completely froze over and a wrecker could come in and pick it up. A lesson learned.

We saw no more deer that week. It was too cold and nothing was moving. I returned to college that week but drove back to Hayward early on Friday for the final weekend. It was snowing heavily, and the temperatures had moderated. I stopped at Alexander & McGill's, where my father worked, advising him that I had arrived and would head up to the shack and get all the fires going. As I was leaving, he jokingly asked, "Are you going out to hunt in this stuff?"

I responded, "I may do that for an hour or two. There's plenty of new tracking snow and I just may get on a hot track, shoot a deer, and leave it on the steps for your arrival."

I arrived at the shack about 3 p.m., started the oil burner, and got a roaring fire going in the wood-burning stove. I had been planning to sit there and enjoy the shack and its solitude, but then I decided to take a short walk to see if there was any activity or fresh tracks. I loaded my rifle and was on Chicago Avenue a short time later.

I was inspecting the new snow on the ground to see if there were any fresh deer tracks when I happened to look up. There before me in the heavily falling snow was a huge doe about thirty yards away. I pulled the rifle to my shoulder and killed her with one shot. I quickly field dressed the deer and then realized that I had nothing with me to drag her back to the shack. I had never expected to see a deer and had left my dragging rope and most of my other gear behind. I removed the belt from my pants, tied it around her neck, dragged her back to the shack, and laid her on the steps. About an hour later, it had grown dark and I could see the lights of the Coot coming toward the shack. I sat inside the shack and giggled to myself, awaiting the reaction from the Jolly Boys when they came around the corner of the shack and discovered the deer on the steps. It was an unforgettable moment for me and one that my father talked about for many years after.

Deer Camps of
Like Kind and Quality

The Jolly Boys and Camp No-Hunt had formed a bond from the very beginning of the development of the two deer camps. No-Hunt was a colorful bunch of fun-loving guys that included Carl Benson, Harold Gobler, Bruce McGill, Heinie Collett, Carl Nordquist, Dane Nelson, and Wilbur Shuman. They were a social group, without a serious deer hunter among them. On the first Sunday night of the annual deer season, when No-Hunt would either come to Blue Heaven or we would go to their camp, there was always friendly competition to see who could do the best job of entertaining their visitors and who could serve up the best dinner.

Although the men of Camp No-Hunt were the closest compatriots to the Jolly Boys, there were also multiple other deer camps in our area that deserve to be mentioned. The Jolly Boys and Camp No-Hunt did not have exclusive expertise in operating a successful hunting camp. Almost all camps had their own traditions, colorful names for identification, and their own methods for building memories. Many were on private lands, but a multitude of camps also took advantage of the Recreational Use Permits issued by Sawyer County. Each deer season involved trying to communicate with many of the other camps as the season progressed to obtain reports on the success of the other hunters in the area. This account only scratches the surface of the numerous deer camps that dotted the landscape in our area. A complete accounting could fill a book of its own.

To our immediate west were the hunters of the Silver Dollar Club and Club 27. We didn't know the hunters from the Silver Dollar Club very well but knew they hailed from southern Wisconsin and hunted the county forestlands to their immediate west, so we seldom crossed paths in the woods. Conversely, we would frequently see the hunters of Club 27 in the woods during deer season, as they hunted just to the north of our camp. Often, Darrell Slama or Richard "Son of Beach" Schmitt would stop by Blue Heaven to check out what was hanging on our buck pole and bring us up to date on who had been successful in shooting a deer. To our south just off the Jolly Fisherman Road were several hunters from Minnesota. They called themselves Minnesota Ridge, and we would run into them while hunting in the southern parts of our hunting area. To our east were all of my mother's relatives on Nelson Lake, hunting out of their cabin, which they called Togi Bay. Adjacent to them was Norbert Reisterer and his sons, Ron and Steve. They called their camp Reisterer's Roost. The hunters from Togi Bay and Reisterer's Roost hunted just on the fringes of the hunting area to our east. It wasn't unusual for any of these hunters to show up at our door to wet their whistle and check out what kind of success we were having during the deer hunt.

Farther to our north, situated along the Seeley Fire Lane, the Bushland and Gillis families both had camps. Bushland's consisted of Lloyd Bushland and his son Forrest, along with other relatives and friends. The Gillis camp, called Dynamite Hill, was occupied by brothers Don and Dick Gillis along with their sons, Phil Barnes, and Bob Mockler. To the west of these camps lay Bare-Naked Purgatory Swamp occupied by Ward, Ross, and Rolf Williamson and their friends, Al Fuller and Rollin Swanson. There was also Camp Handicapped, so named because two of its members wore artificial limbs. This camp developed after Bare-Naked Purgatory Swamp disbanded and the camp members included my cousin, JK Dunster, Rolf Williamson, Mike Kelsey, Al Fuller, Tom Graham, and Don Sahs.

One of the larger deer camps in our area was The Shack: a concrete hunting cabin built by cement mason Ernie Anderson and originally owned by Walt West, Bud Smith, Shorty Jensen, and Dick Wade. It became a family-oriented deer camp, complete with the luxury of a flush toilet, and was used by more than twenty hunters from the area. Over the decades, the owners became Ward Williamson, Mike Sawyer, Jeff Williamson, and Greg Biskcup. The Shack was well known and popular in the area, and game warden Milt Dieckman would frequently visit the camp with his good friend Jay Reed from the *Milwaukee Journal*, who took photos and wrote stories for his outdoor articles.

I also recall that the Brandt family had a large deer camp that had been in existence for years in the Lost Land Lake area. Another camp, known as Red Ike, consisted of Haywardites Jack Moreland, Nate DeLong, Dick Swiler, George Rhenstrand, Basil Eastman, and Gordy Skamser. Word had it that Red Ike actually had a television set to watch football games during deer season. It made one wonder how serious these guys were about the hunt.

During the early years of Blue Heaven, Vern Inhoff had been a frequent guest of the Jolly Boys at various functions that were held at the camp. Vern was impressed with the design and success of Blue Heaven; so much so that in 1970 Vern joined forces with his son Gary to construct their own hunting camp, along with Bob and Rob Labarre, Arnie Anderson, Phil Barnes, Rick Anderson, Dave Henning, and Don Primley Senior and Junior. They copied the design of Blue Heaven in the construction of their hunting camp, which was a great source of pride for the Jolly Boys.

Many of these deer camps are no longer in existence today. The termination of the Recreational Use Permits on December

ANNUAL MEETING OF HUNTER"S INC. 1957

The first annual meeting of the Hunter's Inc. was held at the C.V. Benson
residence on Dec. 27. 1957 at 8:00 P.M. with President Benson presiding.
Members present were Carl Nordquist and Carl Benson. Members absent were:
Harold Gobler, Orville Nelson, Harland Collett, Bruce McGill and Wilbur
Shuman.

It was unanimously agreed that as C.V.Benson was the only successful male
(Buck) with Horns Deer Slayer among the memebers of the Hunters Inc. he be
President and the following slate of officers be sworn in office for the
year 1957-58 and have full jurisdiction at the Lodge in Totogatic.
1. C.V.Benson--President
2. Harold Gobler--Past President, Secretary and Treasurer
Orville (Dane) Nelson--Past, Past President
4. Bruce (Nippy) McGill--Never, Never President
5. Harland (Heinie) Collett--Bull Cook and custodian of the slot machine
6. Carl (Reddy) Nordquist--Has gun-will travel
7. Wilbur Shuman--Chief Jeep Driver--As hunter, time will tell.

The following change in By Laws was adopted:
1. Snoring must be limited to President Benson only.
2. Placing of bombs under toilet seat prohibited.
3. Gurgling of Intoxicating Liquors prohibited before breakfast on
Saturday, Sunday, Monday, Tuesday, Wednesday, Thursday and Friday. Holi
days and Goblers Birthday excepted. Liquor for gurgling purposes to
be furnished by gurgler--(Heinie).
4. All Hunters (including McGill) to be out offcamp and ready for
action by 11:30 A.M. on opening day of season
5. Card playing POSITIVELY prohibited during the hous of 4A.M. to
11 A.M. Adverse weather conditions may alter this decision of President
Benson.
6. All members to remain seated and perfectly quiet during the
following T.V. Programs:
1. Gunsmoke, 2. Wyatt Earp, 3. Have Gun Will Travel
4. Sheriff of Cochise, 5. Colt 45
7. Nordquist (Have Gun Will Travel) be permitted to have Jam and Preserve
at his discretion.
McGill (nippy) to operate, Maintain and have full supply of gas, oil,
and batteries for Kohler Plant (Light and Power) at all hours.
9. Dane (Carpenter Nelson) to have Deer (Buck) Rack ready on demand.
10. Past President Gobler (GRUB) to bring back alive Water Buffalo
seen by him somewhere in the Totogatic on or about Nov. 22, 1957.
11. Wilbur (Broken Ribs) Shuman to carry adequate liability insurance
(Doctors and Hospitalization) while lying in bunk.

Full cooperation by all Members to the best of their ablity is expected
at all times and under all ciecumstances.

APPROVED AND SEALED

C V Benson

C.V.Benson--President

31, 2010, meant the camps were no longer allowed to exist on
county forestlands. The hunters that occupied them moved on
to hunt elsewhere, but the memories of those camps will long
be remembered.

Deer Camps Remembered

Adder was the night owl of our hunting camp and a great story-teller. He took pride in relating stories of the deer camps of yester-year that could be found in our area during the Great Depression and just before World War II. He had witnessed many of them and would sit at the table by the light of the Aladdin lamp late into the night, smoking his pipe, sipping on a snifter of brandy, and reciting his memories of visiting those camps when he was a young man. He would describe in great detail the hardships hunters endured back then, and we'd listen intently to his tales.

The deer camps of that era were very crude by today's stan-dards. The hunters that occupied them all had the same mission: to slay a deer and bring it home to help feed their families. They showed up with their well-oiled deer rifles and boots, wearing an assortment of worn, heavy wool clothing, and had usually walked to the camp carrying the supplies they needed in a knapsack on their back. There were no shared meals back then. For the most part, everyone came as an individual hunter and the only food shared would be fried venison heart or liver if someone was for-tunate enough to shoot a deer. The hunters brought their own personal supplies. It was simple fare, consisting of dried or canned meat, salt pork, beans, coffee, a few seasonings, lard for frying, and maybe a little moonshine or tobacco to enjoy before bedtime. The camps all had names, and most were named after local landmarks.

Some camps did not have a specific owner. They had been built in the past by loggers or trappers for shelter and had been left abandoned for the use of anyone who wished to stay there.

The hunters mostly slept in a shelter made of logs with a dirt floor. The floor would become muddy as the heat from the stove thawed the ground inside the shack. These buildings were constructed with the materials available from the surrounding woods. They were indeed what one would consider a "hunting shack." They had no frills, and the furnishings inside were sparse or nonexistent. Ceilings were low and the bunks had wood slats to hold straw, which was used to cushion and insulate the bunk. No one had sleeping bags back then. They used wool blankets. A small pot-bellied stove provided heat, which also served as a cooking surface that was shared by all. Frequently, the hunters would just eat from a pot or pan rather than using a plate. There was no electricity or running water. The lighting was provided by oil-burning lamps or candles, and water was obtained from a nearby creek or by melting snow. Even if the appropriate facilities had been available, it was too cold to bathe in these hunting camps and there was no privacy in which to do so.

The hunters would be in the woods from the crack of dawn until it became too dark to see. They spent their evenings mending their hunting gear, reading, or discussing the day's hunt or tales of trophy bucks taken in years past. Most would sit or lie around in their wool underwear while their hunting clothes dried out near the pot-bellied stove. During those times, it was a brotherhood formed out of necessity and a common quest.

When I was in my early teens, I had the opportunity to experience one of those old hunting camps. My friends and I had discovered a shack while partridge hunting north of Hayward in the Totogatic Flowage area. It was located in the hardwoods about a half mile off Highway 27 about twelve miles north of town and had been built into the side of a small hill with large white pine logs. It had two small windows in the front, and the only door was still secure and hanging from leather straps that were used for hinges. We checked out the interior and found four double bunks, a handmade table with several stools, and a pot-bellied stove that appeared to be fully functional. It was dry inside, and it seemed that the tar-papered roof had not been leaking. Everything appeared to still be in reasonably good condition and habitable.

We decided it would be fun to camp out there for a night, and several of my buddies and I talked my dad into giving us a ride up to the area the following weekend with our supplies. It was late fall, and the leaves had fallen off the trees. The days were mild, but at night the temperature fell into the low thirties. We planned to spend the day bird hunting in the area, stay overnight in the old shack, and have my father pick us up and return to town the next morning. We hiked into the old deer camp carrying our shotguns and sleeping bags, along with Kool-Aid, hot dogs, and canned beans for our supper, and some candles for light at night. We all thought it was going to be a great adventure to spend a night in this old deer camp.

On arrival, we gathered enough firewood to start a fire in the stove and stockpiled enough wood to keep the place heated overnight. We cleaned up the place the best that we could. Although we saw evidence of a few deer mice, we weren't concerned about their presence, as we knew we could do little to rid the place of them. I selected one of the upper bunks, unrolled my sleeping bag on the straw, and jumped up in the bunk to try it out. I closed my eyes momentarily and thought about what it must have been like to live in this old log cabin deep in the woods years ago. As I lay there, I heard some rustling close to me where the wall and roof joined together. I assumed I had invaded a space where some mice were nested but decided to have a closer look. There, lying about a foot away from me on the top sill of the wall where it met the roof rafters, was a four-foot-long bull snake. I shot out of that bunk like a launched missile and quickly pointed out my discovery to my companions. We immediately agreed that, given my discovery, it might not be wise for us to try to sleep overnight in those old bunks. The bull snake, we realized, ruled that old hunting shack, and we were the intruders. He had found shelter and had plenty of deer mice to dine on, and we had no business attempting to invade his established territory. We gathered our gear, hiked about two miles to a resort on Nelson Lake, and called my father, asking to be retrieved. My father didn't say much on his arrival, but I could tell by the smile on his face that he was thinking we shouldn't have allowed that snake to change our plans. However, I had already made up my mind that I was not willing to spend my night cuddled up with a bull snake.

The Boot Rack

They say that necessity is the mother of invention. Such was the case in the mid-1960s when Adder and I came up with a solution for all the wet boots scattered on the shack floor during the overnight hours.

The hunting boots back then were what people called "packs." They had rubber bottoms with leather uppers that laced. A hunter could purchase felt insoles for them, but after he spent a day stomping around in the woods, the inside of his boots would always be wet from sweating feet or stepping in water. At night, the hunters piled their boots by the oil burner in an effort to dry them out, but it was futile. In the morning, the insides of the boots were always still wet and also cold from sitting on the uninsulated floor overnight.

After the evening's activities had concluded, the light plant would be turned off and replaced by the soft glow of Aladdin lamps, which we lit and placed on the table. Many of the hunters would retire for the evening and head for their bunks, exhausted from the day's activities and looking forward to a good night's sleep and the next day's hunt. But not Adder, the camp night owl. This was his favorite time of the day. He would pour a small shot of brandy, settle in at his favorite spot at the table, and soak in the ambience of the deer camp. Who could blame him? The Aladdin lamps gave off a soothing, dim yellow light. The only sounds were the wood in the stove gently snapping, the tea kettles on the back of the stove barely hissing, and a few of the hunters gently snoring in their bunks. The shack was warm and cozy. It was a little slice of heaven at Blue Heaven.

Adder was the patriarch of the hunting camp, and everyone took his council seriously. He was a force to be reckoned with at the poker table, and he usually ended up as one of the winners at the end of the evening. One such evening, during the middle of deer season in the mid-1960s, Adder had taken his usual place at the table and invited me to stay up and have a nightcap with him. We had finished an excellent evening dinner of garlic-laced pork roast complemented by my father's squash and mashed potatoes, and Merle had made his famous oyster dressing and gravy. Everyone else had already crawled into their bunks. I poured myself an after-dinner drink and sat down at the table with him. We shared stories of the events of that day and were enjoying the dim light of the Aladdin lamps when Adder decided that he should put more wood in the stove. As he walked by the oil burner next to the woodstove, he tripped over one of the many boots that were lined up around the burner. He muttered a few swear words, finished the task of putting more wood on the fire, and returned to the table with a disgusted look on his face.

Adder said to me, "We have to do something about all the boots in here. This place is too small for everyone leaving their boots lying around." I agreed and told him that I had been thinking about that issue for the past couple of years. I went on to say that what we needed was a boot rack hung in the rafters high above the oil burner and woodstove to store and dry all the boots. It's common knowledge that heat rises and cold air falls. Even though our shack is not insulated, the woodstove provides great warmth, with the inside shack temperature frequently reaching eighty degrees or more. At night, the small oil burner keeps the interior temperature from reaching the freezing mark, but in the morning, the interior temperature is forty-five or fifty degrees.

That night on a piece of scratch paper, Adder and I designed and invented the camp boot rack. Adder was an excellent carpenter and had a woodworking shop in his basement at home. We created a simple design. Large spikes would be hammered into predrilled holes about three inches apart in an eight-foot-long two-by-four. The nail heads of the spikes would then be sawed off with a hacksaw, and the two-by-four would be nailed or wired up in the rafters above the stoves. Boots could then be inserted and hung upside down between the spikes.

Adder returned to camp the Friday after Thanksgiving with the newly constructed boot racks. He had made three of them. Each rack could hold up to eight pairs of boots. We installed the boot racks that afternoon, and each hunter slid his wet boots into

The boot rack with about sixteen pairs of boots hanging upside down above the wood cookstove and oil burner

the rack at the end of that day's hunt along with his wet gloves and wool socks. The next morning, everyone had dry, warm boots. The invention and success of the boot rack is still a topic of conversation today when we hang up our boots for the night.

The following deer season, Adder brought in eight individual wood storage lockers. He had constructed them to be used by the hunters to store their surplus gear, which had previously been stowed in the bunk area. He had secretly obtained the necessary measurements during the previous deer season. Six of the lockers were stacked into one unit, and the other two were stacked in another. There was much debate over who would use which locker, and the Jolly Boys went into "executive session" to make that decision. This innovation was welcomed by all and allowed each hunter to have easy access to all his spare equipment and small personal belongings. On occasion, the Jolly Boys held locker inspections to ensure that everyone's locker was orderly and contained the essential goods for a successful deer hunt. There is more than one kind of "boot camp."

Nightly Card Games

During the long, dark evening hours of deer season, many hunting camps pass the time with card games of poker or cribbage. Blue Heaven was no exception. The game of choice would normally be poker, but on occasion there would be only two or three hunters in camp at night, and cribbage requires only two to four players.

From the beginning, the Jolly Boys decided that any card games played at the shack needed to have limitations and rules to keep things from getting out of control. The last thing anyone wanted to see was someone losing or winning a lot of money at the card table and bad feelings developing between the hunters. The evening card games were to provide entertainment and camaraderie until it was time to serve the evening meal. The Jolly Boys wanted the card games to be friendly, and there were shack rules concerning the stakes and rules of play. If a shack rule did not specifically address the situation, the Book of Hoyle, a book written by Edmond Hoyle outlining specific rules for poker games and cribbage, would be consulted.

The first rule addressed stakes. The Jolly Boys would play "nickel-dime" poker, meaning that each poker chip equaled five cents, and the poker chips would be purchased from an individual designated as the banker for the evening. The ante and maximum bet on seven-card games would be limited to five cents. On five-card games, the stakes were limited to ten cents for the ante and bets. A maximum of only three raises would be allowed in each betting session. Keeping the stakes to nickels and dimes would restrict winnings or losses to around ten dollars per evening for a player, no matter how lucky or unlucky they might be on any particular evening. The Jolly Boys recognized that everyone at the poker table had different incomes, and they wanted to include and encourage the younger hunters to also play in the poker games.

To assist the inexperienced players, a rule was established that "the cards speak for themselves." At the end of each game, the players who had remained in the game would turn their cards over and declare their hands. On occasion, an inexperienced player would declare his hand and one of the more experienced players would recognize that the hand being shown was actually higher than what the player had declared. Had this rule not been applied, there would have been many a winning hand thrown in by the inexperienced player and the pot lost by the actual winner.

The poker games would be "dealer's choice." Everyone had a favorite game that they thought they had the best chance at winning, so a wide variety of games could be played on any given evening. The evening poker game would start as soon as all of the hunters had come in from the woods, changed clothes, and put out snacks for everyone's enjoyment. Everyone playing would normally purchase about two dollars' worth of chips from the banker, and whoever had been the big winner the previous evening had the duty to deal out cards faceup to everyone playing until a jack appeared. Whoever received the first jack had the privilege of dealing the first game.

There isn't enough space in this book to describe all of the various card games that we've played at the poker table at our hunting camp over the years, and most of these games and their descriptions can be found in any good book on poker. However, we do play some exciting and unusual games. The most frequently played games at our poker table are five-card draw with deuces

Poker game with Dennis and Russ Clagett, Adder, Marvin, Merle, and Bob, who is preparing to deal the next hand

wild and a game called Baseball, which is a seven-card stud game with threes and nines wild. In Baseball, a player who is dealt a four faceup gets a free card dealt facedown, and a player has to pay extra for a wild three if it is dealt faceup. Baseball is one of our favorite games, and the winner can win a pot worth several dollars when the game is concluded. We also play a game called Dime Store, which is five-card draw with fives and tens wild. Playing poker games with so many wild cards usually requires a rather high hand to win the game, and it's not unusual to have several players holding four of a kind or a straight flush.

On occasion, we will play a five-card game called Spit in the Ocean. The dealer will designate one of the players to call out "Spit" at some point while four cards are being dealt facedown to the players. When the designated person shouts "Spit," the dealer turns up a card from the deck and places it at the center of the table. That card (and all others like it) is wild. The card that was "spit" serves as the fifth card in everyone's hand. A player can draw two cards, and the best five cards in this game wins. We also like a game called 3-3-3. Three cards are dealt faceup, three cards are dealt facedown, and threes are wild.

My favorite poker game is a seven-card stud game called "Low hole card is wild and all others like it." I find it challenging because two cards are dealt facedown, four are dealt faceup, and the seventh and final card is dealt facedown. That final card can change the complexion of your hand and can either make or break your chances of winning, especially if you started the game with a pair of fours dealt to you facedown and then a lower card was dealt to you as the final face-down card. Most people playing this game stick it out to the end, and it usually takes a relatively high hand to win the game. The best five cards of the seven are used when declaring the poker hand. The dealer always carefully monitors this game to make certain that the face-down cards are being carefully separated from the face-up cards and are not commingled.

In the mid-1960s, my father's youngest brother, Bobby Hanson, began to hunt with us, as his hunting group had disbanded and we had a spare bunk for him to occupy. Bobby lived in Superior, Wisconsin, and always referred to himself as "the Superior Card Player." He loved to play poker, and he loved to play cribbage. Bobby was a certified public accountant and had a gift for playing cards well. If you were playing cribbage with him, more often than not he had your hand counted before you even counted it yourself. He would say, "Take your twelve" or "Take your fourteen" while you were still trying to determine how many cribbage points you had in your hand.

When Bobby arrived at camp, he introduced the Jolly Boys and the other hunters to a new poker game that he called Red Dog. In most poker circles, this game is called Guts. It quickly became our favorite game because of its simplicity and the fact that it's a game where one can bluff and end up winning the pot.

Red Dog is dealt by the dealer after calling for an ante of a nickel, dime, or even a quarter from each player. Each player is trying to win the money in the pot. Two cards are dealt to each player facedown. The big advantage to this game is that the deck has fifty-two cards and each player receives only two cards, so a large group can play together. Also, one does not require a great deal of poker knowledge or skill to play Red Dog, as the game is simply won by the player having the two best cards. Suits and runs don't count in this game, a pair of aces is the highest hand, and any pair is a great hand, as is a high face card such as a king.

Once all the players have their two cards, each player takes a turn saying either "in" or "out," starting clockwise to the left of the dealer. Then, every other player has the opportunity to declare in or out, which is done around the table back to the dealer. If only one player has declared himself or herself in, that player wins the money in the pot, the game is over, and the deal passes to the next player. If two or more stay in the game, the player with the highest hand wins the pot and the others that stayed in have to match the pot. If everyone at the table has declared to be out, the dealer cannot say "in" and win the pot unless the dealer has an ace or higher in his or her hand. If the dealer doesn't have an ace, the dealer reshuffles the cards and redeals, and the game starts anew. Often a player might stay in with just a king and another card or even a smaller hand, attempting to bluff and win the pot.

The players sitting the closest to the dealer after most of the players have declared whether they are in or out have the best opportunity to bluff if no one is staying in. Frequently, everyone will declare that they are out, and the only two remaining to declare in or out are the dealer and the person sitting to the dealer's immediate right. The player sitting on the dealer's right often will try to "buy" the pot by bluffing and will stay in even though the player may only be holding two very low cards. If the dealer also has a low hand, the dealer will usually fold rather than taking the chance, to "keep the other player honest" and calling the bluff.

There's a real kicker to this game: there are no ties. If two winning players have exactly the same hand, such as an ace and a ten, they both lose even though they might have the highest hands, and they have to match the pot. If more than two players are in consistently, the pot can double or even triple in size very quickly. The Jolly Boys, in keeping with their philosophy of keeping the poker stakes reasonable, quickly recognized this and established a two-dollar win-or-lose limit for the players. As a result, the most anyone can pull from the pot after a win is two dollars, and the most anyone has to put in if they lose is two dollars. The only way the pot can be "cleared" is if only one person stays and the amount in the pot is less than two dollars. If several players are constantly staying in, one game of Red Dog can last for a very long time.

At the shack, everyone looks forward to the nightly poker games, as they not only provide a great source of entertainment, but are also a good time to share stories of the day's hunt, plan the next day's hunt, talk politics, or discuss a variety of other topics while the cards are being shuffled. In my opinion, shack life is 80 percent of deer hunting. I am also of the opinion that the nightly card games are 80 percent of shack life.

The poker game will usually last from about five in the afternoon until eight or nine in the evening. When the gang mutually decides on the appropriate time to terminate the poker game and have a songfest or set the table for the evening meal, one of the players will be designated to be the last dealer before everyone cashes in their chips. That person is given the honor of dealing one final game, called Showdown.

Showdown is a great way to end an evening of poker. It provides an opportunity for someone who has lost at cards that evening to recover some of his losses or for one of the winners to increase his winnings. By agreement between all the players at the table, an ante of twenty-five or fifty cents (and sometimes up to a dollar) is placed in the center of the table. The designated dealer will then deal each player five cards, one at a time, and all faceup for everyone to see. When the deal is completed, the player with the highest poker hand showing wins the Showdown pot.

Following dinner and cleaning up the kitchen area, the majority of the Jolly Boys and several other hunters would head for their bunks, but there were always a few die-hards who wanted to stay up for a bit longer for a "night cap" and engage in a game or two of cribbage by the light of the Aladdin lamps. Cribbage was also played late in the afternoon before everyone sat down for the nightly poker game. As with poker, the Jolly Boys designated shack rules for the stakes of the cribbage games. They established that the winner would be entitled to receive twenty-five cents, and fifty cents for "skunk." They maintained a rule that if a player had a blank hand, the player would have to pay a ten-cent penalty to every other player. Now, the blank-hand payment has been abolished from the rules, as everyone eventually agreed that it wasn't right to penalize players for not having any points in their cribbage hand.

One stormy day back in the mid-1970s, six of us had returned to camp by midafternoon because the mixture of heavy, wet snow and freezing rain made it almost impossible to hunt. We decided that it would be a great afternoon to stay in the shack and just relax. Dennis Clagett opted to crawl into his upper bunk with a candle and a book he had brought along to read, and listen to the rain on the roof. I was occupying myself by taking care of a few kitchen chores, and the other four guys decided to play a little cribbage while sipping on tap beer until it was time for the poker game to get under way. The cribbage game that ensued was the usual competitive game, with Russ and Bobby as partners taking on my father and Adder. There was much vocalizing in the game, and I noticed that Dennis had come out of his bunk and grabbed a pen and writing pad from the shelf to take back to his bunk. I didn't know what he was up to until later that afternoon, when he showed me his scribbled notes on the pad. Dennis, who had never played a hand of cribbage in his life, had become fascinated with various phrases and comments being made by the four cribbage players as they played the game, and he had written down what he heard, for future reference. I share his comments, slightly edited, with all my fellow cribbage lovers, who will know instantly what each phrase or comment means:

1. Look at the cut that ***hole got!
2. What am I supposed to do with this s***!
3. Sonofabitch. . . . What am I supposed to do with this f****** mess?
4. I have 20. F*** ya. . . .
5. Knock. . . . Knock. . . . Knock. . . . Knock. (The sound of players hitting their knuckles on the table instead of saying "go")
6. Oh, s***!
7. Whose play?!
8. Too f*****' many. . . . (Meaning someone had been dealt a large hand)
9. Whose crib?
10. I need a cut.
11. F***** either way. (Referring to discarding for the crib)
12. What kind of s*** is this?!
13. This is f****** unbelievable!
14. Who dealt this s***?
15. This sucks.
16. What in the f*** are you doing with that card?

Sound familiar?

The Dog Robber

No respectable hunting shack should be without a functional slot machine to entertain the hunters and raise revenue for camp operations. As good fortune would have it, Adder was able to find an old twenty-five-cent slot machine buried in the basement of the old Peoples National Bank. He brought it home and spent countless hours renovating it to make it functional. Fearful that someone would break into the shack and steal this antique, Adder lugged the machine to Blue Heaven each deer season and lugged it back home again for storage when the season had concluded. The Jolly Boys aptly nicknamed it "the dog robber" after the old military term for a general's lackey, who was utilized to fix problems or make them go away.

The Jolly Boys and all their guests at Blue Heaven would pump quarters into it, hoping to hit a jackpot to pay for their hunting trip, but Adder had the slot machine screwed down so tightly that it seldom spit out more than a quarter or two as winnings. The exception was in the mid-1960s, when my dad's brother Bobby and his friend George paid a visit to the camp just as we were about to sit down for brunch. Being good hosts, we welcomed them, made them each a Bloody Mary, and invited them to join us. George walked over to the slot machine and started putting quarters into it and pulling the lever. On his third quarter, the slot machine that never paid spilled its guts, and quarters came flowing out. All of us were in disbelief. He had hit the mother lode and had the unmitigated gall to ask for a coffee can to haul away his winnings. All the Jolly Boys were in shock that George didn't return a portion of his winnings to them. Instead, he had walked away with revenue that had been meant for the shack operations fund. It goes without saying that my father's brother was chastised for bringing George into our hunting camp, and George was banned for life.

Lost in the Woods, 1965

In the fall of 1964, Merle showed up driving a new toy that had been given to him by a close friend. It was called a Tri-Scat, a three-wheeled motorized tricycle powered by a five-horsepower engine, with two large rear tires and a smaller front tire. It sat very low to the ground and was one of the forerunners of the all-terrain vehicles that would be flooding the recreational market in the years to come. We put the Tri-Scat into service immediately, hauling supplies into the camp and dragging deer back to the shack during deer season. It could transport only one person and didn't perform very well in the snow, but it served its purpose and could avoid all the mud holes in the road leading into the shack.

The Jolly Boys used the Tri-Scat on a rescue mission in 1965 to locate one of our hunters who had gotten lost. My father and Merle had grown up with Sammy Helms in Hayward. The three of them had all enlisted in the navy during World War II, and Sammy became an aviator. After the war ended, Sammy elected to make the navy his career and became close friends with another aviator, Robin "Bob" Larson. For a number of years, Sammy and Bob would fly into Hayward for the fishing season opener in a navy Beechcraft Super 18, a very loud two-engine airplane. They would always "buzz" Hayward on their arrival, and my dad and Merle would rush out to the airport to pick them up.

In 1965, Sammy couldn't make it to Wisconsin for deer-hunting season, so Bob was invited to come up by himself. Bob was an avid hunter, known for taking frequent trips out West to hunt mule deer, elk, and other large game. He was also an avid fisherman who owned a small cabin in Canada, spending much of his free time fishing up there in the summer. He certainly wasn't a stranger to the woods, and we all regarded him as a part of our group and felt he would be a welcome addition at the shack.

Bob arrived early Friday afternoon to help haul in supplies and get the shack opened up for deer season. At about 3:30 that afternoon, he decided to take a short walk to see if he could locate Merle's deer stand, the Birch, in order to scout the area for deer signs in the snow that had fallen a few days before our arrival. By 4:30, it was dark and Bob wasn't back. Several of us went outside and shouted his name, hoping he would hear us, but we didn't get a response. We were all getting very concerned, as he should have been back before dark and we knew that he had left lightly dressed, with no rifle, flashlight, or compass. About 5 p.m., we fired a couple of shots into the air, hoping he would hear the gunshots, get his bearings, and find his way back. We then took the Jeep and drove down to the area of the Birch. We did find his tracks in the snow where he had entered the woods, but there was no sign of him and no response when we yelled his name. Knowing that Merle was arriving shortly with the Tri-Scat, we went back to the shack to organize a search party.

When Merle and my dad showed up around 6:30 that evening, we informed them that Bob was apparently lost in the woods without a flashlight or compass. Merle dressed in his warm hunting clothes and left camp about 7 p.m. with Adder's son Philip. Their mission was to locate Bob's tracks and follow them by Tri-Scat. They returned about 8:30 that evening with Bob in tow. He was cold, hungry, and very thirsty, but no worse for the wear.

We learned that when Bob got turned around in the woods and realized he was lost, he decided to do the smart thing and stay where he was, build a fire, and wait for us to find him. Although he had heard us firing our rifles, he had no way to respond to us and was fearful of falling and injuring himself if he attempted to walk through the woods in the dark. That evening, Bob made "mooseballs" from moose hamburger that he had brought with him from a moose he had shot in Canada that fall. We all enjoyed a very late dinner and gave thanks that things had turned out well. We managed to fill a couple of party tags that season but were unsuccessful in getting any bucks. Still, we declared the season a success, as everyone had returned from camp safely.

Target Practice, 1966–1967

By the deer season of 1966, the Jolly Boys had perfected their signature style of hunting and entertaining while at deer camp. Once again, the Jolly Boys hosted a huge party on the first Sunday evening of the hunt. Twenty people crammed into that little cabin for an evening of cocktails, deer stories, and a lot of singing. A standing prime rib roast was served for dinner, complemented by baked potatoes, Shack Peas, salad, and a side dish made with sautéed mushrooms, green peppers, and onions. That year had been a buck-only, party-permit season, and although deer weren't plentiful in our area, we had still managed to down two bucks and a party doe for camp meat.

The following year was one that my father would never forget. At that time, I was employed as a young rookie cop, working as a patrolman for the Eau Claire Police Department at night so I could take college courses during the day. I had been unable to get off work for deer season until midnight of the evening before opening day. Thanks to all the adrenaline running through me in anticipation of the big hunt, I had no problem staying awake for the two-hour drive from Eau Claire up to the hunting shack in the wee morning hours. I stumbled my way into the shack in pitch darkness carrying all my hunting gear. Almost everyone was sound asleep on my arrival, but my father greeted me as I crawled into my bunk about 3 a.m. I was hoping for at least a couple of hours of sleep before the alarm clock sounded. At 5 a.m., everyone awoke to the horrible blaring of Merle attempting to play "Reveille" on a bugle that he had smuggled in. He had no problem drowning out the alarm clock, which had also begun to ring to summon us to the hunt.

It was going to be a great day for hunting. The temperature was relatively mild, with very little wind, and about four inches of snow covered the ground. My father announced that he was going to go up past the Little Rocks and position himself on a stump overlooking a large green swamp just west of the Big Rock. I told him that I would hunt just north of him and attempt to push some deer in his direction. About midmorning, I heard three shots from the area where he had posted himself and headed in that direction. I found him sitting on a stump, with a big cigar in the corner of his mouth. When I reached him, I whispered, "Did you get him?" He took the cigar from his mouth and whispered back, "Nope. Nice buck. Running full speed. Shot three times and can't figure out how I missed him."

We both headed back to the shack to join the others for our noon brunch. That afternoon, my father decided to go back, reposition himself on his stump, and sit there until it got dark. About 4 p.m., I heard another three shots coming from his area, but there was no whistling or any other signals indicating he needed help, so I didn't walk over to his area. When we met up a short while later back at deer camp, I asked him, "Was that you shooting again?" He responded, "Had a standing buck that had walked up within seventy-five yards of me. Shot at him three times and he finally turned and ran away." I could tell he was dismayed, as he was an excellent shot and seldom missed. Even though I already knew the answer, I asked him if he had sighted in his deer rifle prior to deer season. He replied, "Too busy for that."

I put up a target, took his .30-30, and fired three shots. All three bullets struck the target high and to the right about two feet off-center at fifty yards. He had somehow bumped his rear sight and had shot over the top of the two deer that he had seen that day. A lesson learned. Always test-fire your deer rifle before opening day.

The Coot

Every year, the most difficult part of getting the camp ready for deer season would be hauling in the supplies from the highway to the hunting shack on the three-quarter-mile logging road. The road was almost always wet, with deep mud holes, and in a near-impassable condition. Would we get stuck? Would one of the old Jeeps have mechanical problems? Would the road be littered with fallen trees? On numerous occasions, our arrival at camp would be delayed for any of these reasons, but the Jolly Boys always showed optimism and someone would quip, "It keeps other hunters and the game wardens from wandering back in here." Transportation in and out of the camp was a constant issue, and the shack log reflects that in numerous entries. All of this would change with the arrival of the Coot.

Merle had become acquainted with a summer resident named Adrian Faase, who was from Omaha, Nebraska. Adrian and his wife, Flowell, had a summer home on nearby Cable Lake. Merle and Gloria became very close friends with Adrian and Flowell, and Merle enjoyed showing off Blue Heaven to them. Adrian and Flowell were guests for a dinner party at the shack in the fall of 1959, and they experienced firsthand the transportation challenges of the muddy logging road.

Adrian owned a company in Omaha called SnowCo, which manufactured a variety of farm equipment and trailers. In the

The Coot's maiden voyage into Blue Heaven in the fall of 1968

mid-1960s, Adrian was contacted by a company that had designed a new four-wheel all-terrain vehicle that they were calling the Coot. They needed a trailer to transport this newly designed vehicle and SnowCo was awarded the contract. In order for Adrian to design the trailer, the manufacturer provided SnowCo with one of its machines. After the trailer was designed, built, and put into production, the Coot manufacturer informed Adrian that he could keep the Coot. The first thought in Adrian's mind was that it would be the perfect vehicle to traverse the muddy road into the hunting shack. In the summer of 1968, Adrian transported the Coot and its trailer to Cable and gave it to Merle as a gift.

The Coot is about the size of a small WWII jeep without a cab or a hood. It's a full-time four-wheel-drive vehicle with two separate body sections that articulate, which allows all four wheels to be in contact with the ground at all times. It isn't powered by a regular vehicle engine. It came equipped with an 18-horsepower Tecumseh engine, and the drive system is powered through a centrifugal clutch, very similar to a snowmobile. The front section of the Coot has a bench seat and provides room for only the driver and one passenger. However, the rear portion is designed to carry cargo or up to four passengers. In later years we added a small trailer that can be pulled to haul additional cargo.

The Coot was geared for power and could easily push over a four-inch aspen tree and drive through heavy brush. It was built to last, with a laminated all-steel frame welded to a 16-gauge steel skin. It is heavy and almost indestructible, and it feels like driving a small tank through the woods. Coots were also designed to be amphibious, much like the WWII "Ducks." We once took ours for a test-drive on a lake and although the tires only generated a speed of a couple of miles per hour, and the vehicle was difficult to steer and maneuver, it did indeed float. The Coot had low gear and high gear for forward movement and one reverse speed.

Although this was the perfect piece of equipment to navigate the logging road, the Coot did have a few design drawbacks. It wasn't equipped with brakes; one simply took his foot off the accelerator and allowed it to roll to a stop. Normally, this was not a problem, but I recall one incident when we were hauling firewood and going up a hill in high gear. The Coot was losing power and coming to a stop, and in our attempt to move the transmission into low gear, the Coot began to roll rapidly backward. It was a harrowing ride until we came to a stop at the bottom of the hill, and we were thankful that the incident hadn't resulted in any injuries. From that day on, we made certain that we had the Coot in low gear before ascending or descending a hill with a full load.

Another issue was turning radius. Although the Coot has a steering wheel and steers like a car, the turning radius is very limited, as the front wheels will rub up against the body of the vehicle

Leaving Blue Heaven on the Coot after a day spent at the shack

when attempting to turn in small circles. It therefore is necessary to plan turns well in advance, similar to an 18-wheeler turning a sharp corner. There is also no suspension on a Coot. When Merle operated the Coot, he did so at one speed: wide open! Whenever we ran over a log or rock, driver and passengers alike would bounce up off their seats and come crashing down with a jolt. Frequently, the ride would be painful, and everyone pleaded for a slow ride when Merle was behind the wheel.

In the mid-1980s, they stopped manufacturing the Coot, but of those that were built, many are still in operation today, including ours. It has been mechanically rebuilt several times over the course of its service to our hunting camp and continues to be completely functional.

Since 1968, the Coot has been our primary source of transportation and has hauled countless hunters and their gear, deer, and camp supplies. There's no telling how many tons of cargo it has hauled. It has been an all-weather and all-terrain vehicle, and we've equipped the four wheels with chains for added traction. The only time the Coot has been stuck is when the driver has high-centered on frozen dirt above the ruts in the road. Today, we use four-wheel-drive four-wheelers in addition to the Coot, since four-wheel-drive pickups and SUVs still get stuck trying to traverse the mud holes to the shack.

The Bunny Girls Entertain, 1968

The Jolly Boys made no shack log entries for deer season 1968, which nonetheless turned out to be one to remember. The pull-down window shade that records all the deer kills indicates that we were successful in harvesting five deer that season. I shot a six-point buck at the Big Rock and also shot two large does. A couple of the other hunters were also successful in bagging a deer.

My father called me a few weeks before the season opener, asking me to learn how to play "Bye Bye Blackbird" on my trumpet and to bring the instrument up to the hunting shack on opening weekend. I had played the trumpet in high school and had been actually quite proficient on it back then, but it was now buried in a closet somewhere and I hadn't touched it for years. I asked my dad what was going on. All he would tell me was that the Jolly Boys were planning some special entertainment for when the hunters from Camp No-Hunt arrived on Sunday night for the annual party between the two deer camps. It was a secret and he wouldn't say any more. It took some effort, but I learned to play the song and brought my trumpet up to deer camp. After the opening day of hunting was over, my dad asked that I play "Bye Bye Blackbird" for him and the other Jolly Boys. I pulled out my trumpet and played the song. It met with their approval, and they thanked me for learning to do it. But the rest of us hunters were still in the dark as to what the Jolly Boys were up to.

Sunday arrived, and after hunting until about three that afternoon, we all came back to camp early to prepare for the big party with Camp No-Hunt. We cleaned the shack, stowed our personal gear, put snacks out on the counter, and prepped a huge prime rib roast to be put into the oven with scrubbed baked potatoes. In addition to the members of Camp No-Hunt, many others had been invited to this party, so we knew that the shack would be wall-to-wall with people and we would have to take turns at the dinner table. At least twenty people were in attendance for the party that evening.

Everyone arrived. Cocktails were served, snacks were consumed, and deer stories were told. It was definitely a party atmosphere. At some point my dad and the other three Jolly Boys disappeared into the bunk area and pulled the curtains behind them. We all wondered what they were up to and heard lots of laughter and commotion going on behind the curtains. A few minutes later my dad stuck his head out from behind one of the curtains and motioned for me to join them. When I entered the bunk area, their secret became known to me. The four of them were dressed as Playboy Bunnys. My mother had designed the bunny costumes by stuffing old bras and sewing a large bunny tail on the backside of each Jolly Boy's underwear. She had also made each man a headband with rabbit ears. The four of them stood there in their costumes, dyed blue in honor of Blue Heaven, their unshaven chests and legs for all the world to see. It was showtime.

My father told me to grab my trumpet from my bunk area and go out and play "Bye Bye Blackbird." I did so, and the four Jolly Boys parted the curtains and came out of the bunk area kicking up their legs in unison and singing a song they had written to the melody of the song I was playing:

Marv, Adder, Merle, and Kenny during their bunny girl show for
Camp No-Hunt

Sooooooooooo...

Back your a** against the wall, here we come, balls and all.
Welcome, No-Hunt....

Wiggle your t*** and shake your a**, grab yourself an
empty glass. Welcome, No-Hunt....

We bunny girls are here to please you, with our costumes
we will tease you....

Sooooooooooooo...

Back your a** against the wall, here we come, balls and all.
Welcome, No-Hunt.

The entertainment was a huge success and they were asked
to perform two encores. The event was talked about for years
to come, and to this day no other entertainment or costume or
merriment has matched those antics.

REALI SPAGHETTI

I love spaghetti with a great spaghetti sauce. Served with toasted garlic bread and an Italian salad, and complemented with a fine red wine, it's one of my favorite meals.

My sister, Marilynn, married DeLarry "Larry" Joseph Reali (pronounced "Ree-AL-ee") in 1959. Larry was the son of Carl and Lesla Reali, and the family was of Italian and French heritage. They possessed an Old World recipe for spaghetti sauce that had been kept a family secret for years. It had been passed down from generation to generation, and whenever Larry visited us, we all begged him to make a batch of Reali spaghetti. The process took all day, so we always felt honored when he agreed to spend hours in the kitchen preparing it.

For years I tried to sneak a peek at the ingredients Larry used when he made his family's treasured recipe, but he always knew I was watching and always managed to disguise precisely what he was putting into the sauce. When Larry paid a visit to Blue Heaven in 1969, armed with the ingredients to make a spaghetti dinner for the hunters, I purposely stayed in the shack that afternoon and volunteered to assist him in preparing the famous Reali spaghetti sauce while the others went out to hunt. He finally caved in and shared the secret of the family recipe with me. It is a recipe that needs to be shared with everyone who loves spaghetti as I do. What makes the Reali sauce unique is its pork rib base, which gives the sauce a richness and flavor unlike any other spaghetti sauce. It will serve at least twelve hungry people, and I always make a full batch, as the leftover sauce freezes beautifully and can also be used for lasagna. Preparing the ingredients for the sauce will take about two hours.

Ingredients

1/4 cup plus 1 tablespoon olive oil

4 (12-ounce) cans Contadina (or other "roma style") tomato paste

7 (12-ounce) cans water

4 pounds ground venison or 80/20 ground beef

4 pounds pork ribs cut into 3- to 4-inch pieces

4 large yellow onions

3 (13.25-ounce) cans mushroom stems and pieces

8–10 large cloves fresh garlic

6 tablespoons oregano flakes

3 tablespoons sweet basil flakes

2 tablespoons salt

2 teaspoons black pepper

4 large bay leaves

2 (16-ounce) packages spaghetti

Romano or Parmesan cheese, for garnish

Preparation

You will need a large, heavy duty pot with a lid in which to prepare the sauce. Always use low heat and stir the sauce frequently to keep it from sticking and scorching on the bottom of the pot.

Begin by putting a quarter cup of olive oil in the pot to help keep the sauce from sticking. Add the tomato paste and water to the pot and combine. Heat to a simmer over low heat.

Meanwhile, season the venison by sprinkling with salt and pepper and brown in a frypan. Salt and pepper the pork ribs and slowly brown in a frypan on both sides, using a little olive oil, or brown under the broiler. Once they're browned, drain the excess fat and add the venison and pork ribs to the pot.

Dice the onions, sauté them in the frypan with a little olive oil, and add them to the pot. Drain the mushrooms and add them to the pot. Make certain that you are stirring the sauce all the way to the bottom of the pot frequently.

Peel the garlic cloves and either mince them or use a garlic press and add them to the sauce. Add the oregano, basil, salt, pepper, and bay leaves and stir to combine. Simmer the sauce, covered, over low heat for 4 to 5 hours, stirring frequently.

After the sauce has simmered, the rib meat will start to separate from the bones. Remove the rib meat and bones from the sauce and place in a separate dish. Be careful to remove any stray rib bones from the sauce. Cut up any large pieces of rib meat, return the meat to the pot, and continue to simmer for another 1 to 2 hours. Usually, a dark-colored oily residue from the olive oil and ribs will appear at the top of the sauce after it has simmered 5 to 6 hours. This will be used to lubricate the pasta.

Serving

About 45 minutes prior to serving, fill a large pot with salted water and bring to a boil. Boil the spaghetti according to package directions. When the spaghetti has been cooked al dente, use a pasta strainer to drain the spaghetti of all water but do not rinse the spaghetti. Place the spaghetti back in the pot. Skim about 2 cups of sauce and oily residue from the top of the spaghetti sauce and stir into the cooked spaghetti. This will keep the spaghetti from sticking together and will add another element of flavor to the finished dish. Place the spaghetti on individual plates and serve with abundant sauce on top. Leave the Romano or Parmesan cheese on the table for your guests to garnish as they please. Always warn your guests to be on the lookout for any stray rib bones.

Be prepared for your guests to ask for second or possibly even third helpings of your creation. It's that good! The Reali spaghetti is always complemented with toasted garlic bread and your favorite Italian salad and, of course, an ample supply of merlot or your favorite red wine.

Marriage of the Deer Camps,
1969–1970

During deer season 1969, we had an unoccupied bunk, and Merle invited Dennis Clagett to join us for deer camp. Dennis had recently become Merle's son-in-law and had been a close friend of mine since 1965, when Dennis and I roomed together in college. I was thrilled to have another younger hunter coming up for the hunt, as we needed more movement in the woods to push the deer toward one another. The Jolly Boys were getting older and although they still enjoyed deer hunting, their enthusiasm for being in the woods for the entire day was obviously flagging. Most would rather have been back at the shack playing cribbage than sitting on their deer stands.

Dennis knew little about card playing and had limited skills at the poker table, but he showed himself to be a skilled and patient hunter. During his first season with us, he shot a large doe on opening morning and followed it up later in the week by slaying a huge ten-point buck. His success that year begat friendly competition between the two of us in each succeeding year, and we competed to see who could shoot the biggest buck. Merle's son, John Kimball, also shot his first buck that season, and we considered the hunt to be very fruitful considering the limited number of deer in our area that year.

At the end of the season my father penned an entry in the camp log that summarized the previous nine days:

1969 hunting season commenced Nov. 22nd—Present 1st
weekend were Marv, John H., Bob H., Merle, John D., Dennis
~~Clagett, Adder, Philip—Had T-bones Sat. nite—Ken Sugrue~~
came up to join us Sunday nite to go to Camp No-Hunt. Dennis killed nice doe 1st Sat. for camp meat. John Kimball killed
his 1st buck Sunday. Fork horn—Dennis killed 10 point buck
Tues. Merle, Marv and Dennis dragged it through the north
swamp until after dark. We three and wives stayed overnight.
Merle & Marv stayed Wed. nite. Dennis, John H., John D.,
Larry Reali, Marv, Merle & Adder came out the last Friday
night. Larry made spaghetti—very good—very good season—let's do it again.

Dennis possessed excellent mechanical and electronic skills,
and his expertise in keeping the light plant running smoothly was
immediately utilized by the Jolly Boys, who had struggled with
the light plant for years.

In previous seasons Dennis had hunted with his father, Russell, and another father-son duo in the Hungry Run area of eastern
Sawyer County. It was rugged terrain, and there wasn't a hunting
shack available to them. He informed us that they would enter
the woods before daylight and hunt until noon. They would then
start a small fire to warm up and toast cheese sandwiches over
the fire for their lunch. Usually, the bread ended up burned and
the cheese remained frozen from being carried in their pockets
all morning. They had always hunted that way. They would put
out their fire and then hunt until dark, to return home cold and
tired. Naturally, Dennis fell in love with Blue Heaven and the way
the Jolly Boys ran their deer camp; so much so that the following
year, Dennis asked the Jolly Boys for their permission to invite
his father up to experience shack life.

Well known in the Hayward area, Russell Clagett and his
wife, Betty, along with another couple, co-owned and -operated

Herman's Landing, a very popular resort complete with a full bar and restaurant, on the Chippewa Flowage. Russ was an avid sportsman and an icon in the Hayward resort community. We all thought that he would easily fit in with the rest of us at Blue Heaven.

Dennis and Russ arrived on the Sunday night of the first weekend of the 1970 season, after the rest of us had already been in camp for a couple of days. The two of them decided that even though it was already dark, they would walk in carrying their gear rather than pester any of the Jolly Boys to provide transportation. Camp No-Hunt had already arrived for the annual Sunday night party, and the small hunting shack was full of hunters. The party was in full swing when they arrived, and they both immediately joined in the merriment and the spirit of the evening.

The Jolly Boys had decided that Camp No-Hunt and Blue Heaven should "become wed" to signify the bond that they had developed over the years. The Jolly Boys took Carl Benson, who was the patriarch of Camp No-Hunt, back into the bunk area and dressed him in an old wedding gown, complete with a pillow

Merle presides over the marriage of Carl Benson (the bride from Camp No-Hunt) and Kenny Sugrue (the groom from Blue Heaven).

stuffed into the front of the dress so Carl looked as though he were about nine months' pregnant. Carl was the bride, and Kenny Sugrue, our beloved mayor of Hayward, represented the Jolly Boys as the groom. Merle dressed up as the minister and performed the ceremony at an altar he had thrown together with linens and candles. Adder had the honor of being best man for the groom, and Harold Gobler was Carl's maid of honor. By the time the ceremony ended, there wasn't a dry eye in the place—not from tears of joy or sadness, but from laughter.

Russell, like Dennis, was a perfect fit in our hunting camp. He not only loved to hunt for deer with the rest of us, he also thoroughly enjoyed all of the Jolly Boys' antics in the evening when the hunt was concluded. That deer season formed a relationship that would last twenty-eight years.

VIOLET'S CHILI

During the early years of the hunting shack, it was a challenge for the Jolly Boys and the other hunters in our camp to break away early on the Friday before deer season. Frequently, no one was available to leave for Blue Heaven until late Friday afternoon. As the years passed and vacation time became more available, the majority of hunters in our camp were able to leave by late Friday morning. That was when my mother's chili feed tradition began, one year in the early 1970s.

My parents had the ideal home to entertain a large group of guests. Built in 1910, the house had a large kitchen and attached pantry, and the dining room table sat twelve people. It became the common place for everyone to assemble, and my mother volunteered to serve a noon lunch of chili to all of the hunters before they left for camp. It was always a festive gathering, with the anticipation of the hunt in the air. My father would be at the grocery store, gathering supplies for camp, and several hunters would show up as early as midmorning to handle the other chores, knowing that my mother always had the coffeepot on and tins of delicious cookies sitting out on her kitchen table. When my father came home around noon, she would begin to serve the chili to the hunters seated at the dining room table. Several of the hunters' wives usually came to assist her. There were always large bowls of saltine crackers, toasted garlic bread with butter, and milk or beer to wash everything down. We ate cookies for dessert. Almost everyone had a second helping of chili, and some had even three bowls.

The tradition of the chili feed at my mother's continued until she passed away in 2003. We still hold on to the tradition of the pre–deer season chili feed, but we now have it up at camp on the Friday before deer season. We still use my mother's recipe for the chili.

Ingredients

3 pounds ground venison or 80/20 ground beef
2 large yellow onions, chopped
2 cups chopped celery
1 (46-ounce) jug V-8
2 (28-ounce) cans crushed tomatoes
2 (16-ounce) cans dark red kidney beans
1 (16-ounce) can light red kidney beans
1 (13.25-ounce) can mushroom stems and pieces
2 tablespoons chili powder
1 tablespoon salt
1 tablespoon pepper

Preparation

Brown the venison in a large pot. Add the onion and celery as the meat is cooking. Drain excess fat. Add V8 juice and crushed tomatoes. Drain kidney beans and mushrooms, and add to the pot. Add chili powder, salt, and pepper. Simmer on low heat for 3 hours. Serve with saltines and butter and put chili powder on the table for those wanting additional heat. Chili can be garnished with sprinkles of chopped raw onion, shredded cheddar cheese, and Fritos if desired.

Keeping a Record, the 1970s

When I read through all the entries in the shack log from the 1970s, I am constantly reminded of the importance of the log, which provides a diary and chronological history of the memories and events that have taken place at Blue Heaven year after year. We always kept the log on a shelf, available for anyone in camp to make an entry or just read the contents for their entertainment. It wasn't at all unusual to see one of the hunters reading through the log late at night by candlelight or early in the morning while sipping on a cup of coffee. He would always have a little smile on his face while he was reading, reminiscing about the many good times recorded in the log, which soon became tattered from use.

Multiple entries in the log relate tales of the deer hunt or trips to the shack in the dead of winter while putting up with subzero temperatures or knee-high snow. There are stories of New Year's Eve parties with family and friends; fall and spring frolic parties; snowmobiling and cross-country skiing parties; and trips in the fall and spring to cut wood, make improvements or repairs, and fight the never-ending battles to control the mice and porcupines that didn't want to leave the place alone when we weren't there to protect it. The log always reflected who was there during an event. It leaves one with the impression that a substantial number of people from the Hayward area honored the Jolly Boys with a visit to Blue Heaven at one time or another.

The 1970s produced very few deer for the Jolly Boys and the other hunters at Blue Heaven, but that didn't seem to matter much. As long as one or two deer were slain, everyone seemed happy that we would be able to enjoy venison for the deer season, even if there wasn't much left over to take home to stock our freezers. Party-deer tags were being offered through those years, and even though the Jolly Boys managed to get their share of permits, there were many seasons when they went unfilled.

On November 17, 1973, an entry in the log states that I "killed a nine-point buck and a doe 200 yards east of 'The Can.' Temperature in mid-thirties with tracking snow on ground. Merle prepared a pork roast with dressing, squash, salad and mashed potatoes for dinner after a great poker game and happy hour."

I vividly recall that opening Saturday of deer season, because after I was lucky enough to shoot those two deer and was dressing them out, I could hear a pack of coyotes howling about two hundred yards north of me. Naturally, I grew concerned that after I left the area to get the Coot to haul the deer back to camp, the coyotes would move in and devour the deer. I double-timed it back to the shack to find someone to help me load up the two deer and bring them back to the shack. The only hunter in camp was Adder. He was in his midsixties at that time, and although he wanted to help, he felt that it was beyond his capabilities to do so. I recall how bad I felt for him as he stood there and apologized for not being able to provide any assistance. It was there and then that I realized the Jolly Boys were starting to age. I knew that it was just a matter of time before Blue Heaven would be a camp of older hunters more apt to stay in the shack and play cribbage than tramp the woods looking for deer. I drove the Coot back to where I had shot the deer before the coyotes located them and somehow managed to load them into the Coot by myself and get them safely back to camp.

Just eighteen months later, on February 3, 1975, Kenny Sugrue, the beloved Jolly Boy with the golden singing voice, passed away. The Jolly Boys were then only three, and I became aware that there would be many changes ahead for Blue Heaven in the coming years.

Three Generations, 1980

During the summer and fall of 1980, loggers moved into the woods around Blue Heaven to harvest basswood. The tree-farming trucks with their huge wheels had made a complete mess of all the logging roads in the area, leaving big ruts that quickly filled with water and became mud holes. The Jolly Boys grew concerned about transportation to the shack come deer season, and they hoped for an early freeze that year.

Deer season arrived with very little snow on the ground and temperatures in the midthirties. The road was still a mess. If it hadn't been for the Coot, we would have had no choice but to haul in all of our supplies and gear by hand, as the road into camp was impassable. We had only six hunters in camp for that opening weekend: my father and I, Merle and JK Dunster, and Dennis and Russ Clagett. Adder wasn't there that year for deer season, and only two of the five original Jolly Boys occupied their bunks. It seemed unusual to have only six of us in camp for the opening weekend, because in prior years most of the bunks had always been filled. At the end of the first weekend, the Jolly Boys granted permission for my oldest son, Robin, to come up to hunt. He was thirteen, a part of the future for Blue Heaven, and his being a part of the group was just as important to his grandfather and me as it was to him. Now three generations of Hansons occupied bunks at Blue Heaven and the pride on my father's face was evident.

My oldest son, Robin, thrilled to win his first poker game at Blue Heaven

Rob had been up at Blue Heaven on countless previous occasions, but this was the first time he was allowed to come into deer camp, carry a rifle, and hunt. Although he managed to see a deer and get a shot off at it, he unfortunately missed. I knew he was disappointed, but he took it in stride. Wanting him to get the full flavor of hunting-shack life, my father and I staked him a few dollars so he could participate in the evening poker games. Although he managed to win a couple of hands, it wasn't too long before the rest of the players had all of his money on their side of the table. We all knew that in future seasons, experience and seasoning would make him a great deer hunter and poker player.

The following fall we decided it was time to replace the outhouse that had served us well for more than twenty-five years. The old outhouse had started rotting at the base, and it was just a matter of time before it would topple. One of my friends, Dennis Skare, volunteered to donate an old outhouse that he had out at his lake cabin, and we quickly took him up on the offer. It wasn't in the best condition, but it still had many years of serviceable life left. We loaded it onto the back of my pickup to transport it the twenty miles up to Blue Heaven. Naturally, en route to the shack, we had to drive up and down the main street of Hayward a couple of times to show off our cargo.

When we arrived at the road leading into the shack, I put my truck into four-wheel drive and we began to churn our way through the mud holes with our heavy load. About a hundred yards before reaching the shack, we knew there was one particularly nasty mud hole about fifty yards long that we would have to dodge. Anticipating that we might get mired down in the middle of it, I greatly increased our speed and entered the mud hole going as fast as I could, hoping that I would be able to maintain control of the truck and avoid getting stuck. To my delight and amazement, we made it to the other side, chugged up the small hill, and arrived at the shack. However, when we got out of the

The Skare outhouse, installed at Blue Heaven

truck, we discovered that the outhouse was no longer on the back of the pickup. It was lying back in that nasty mud hole and we had been too attentive to making it through the mud to know it had bounced off. After the laughter died down and with a lot of effort, we were able to retrieve the outhouse from the mud hole and get it up to the shack.

Fortunately, the mishap didn't cause much damage to the little building. Years later, the Skare outhouse would make the trip to a new hunting camp, and it is still in service at Blue Heaven.

On the Run, 1981

During the summer months of 1981, the loggers that had been in our area returned with their trucks to haul out the rest of the logs they had cut, and they used a bulldozer to smooth out most of the logging road leading to our shack. Even the big logging trucks couldn't maneuver through the mud holes that had been created by their tree farmers. Although the road was still in tough shape, we were thrilled to see the improvements, with most of the huge ruts being leveled.

In 1980, the deer herd was expanding to a point where the Wisconsin DNR began to issue "hunter's choice" permits. We also called them "either-sex" permits, as it allowed the hunter fortunate enough to get the permit to shoot either a buck or a doe. If you had the permit, you didn't have to determine if the deer had horns or not before you started shooting. We didn't obtain the coveted permit in 1980, but during the deer season of 1981, Russ and I both obtained a hunter's choice permit. On opening morning, Rob got to shooting at a spike buck but missed it. Later that day, the spike buck came by my stand, and I was more fortunate, managing to bring it down. I collected eight dollars off the deer horns back at Blue Heaven for getting the "first set of nuts," and we tagged the deer with a tag from one of the older hunters in our camp. The following day, Russ filled his either-sex permit by shooting a huge doe, and Dennis dragged a nice six-point buck into camp. We had three deer hanging by the end of opening weekend and rejoiced in the fact that the deer population in our area seemed to be improving.

Not to be outdone for the season by my friend Dennis, I shot an eight-point buck a couple of days later. On the Wednesday morning of that season, it had started snowing quite heavily just as we were all returning to the shack for our noon brunch. By the time we finished eating, there was already several inches of new, heavy, wet snow on the ground. We were all eager to get back into the woods for the afternoon hunt. I decided that I would walk down a new access road that the loggers had made, which went through an area of thick tag alders and aspen saplings. I figured that if I were a deer, I would want to be in that area for shelter when it was snowing heavily. As I began my trek down that road, I marveled at the silence of the snowfall. There was no wind. The air was wet, making it difficult for a deer to smell me, and I could sneak down that road in complete silence. These were ideal hunting conditions, and I thought that I had a good chance of sneaking up on a deer during this snowstorm.

I soon came across tracks in the snow of a deer that had recently crossed the road. There was only a small amount of new snow in the tracks, so I decided to follow it. I was only about thirty yards away from the road in the thickness of the tag alders when I found a deer bed that was so fresh, there was hardly any new snow lying in it. My heart started to beat heavily in my chest as I followed the fresh deer tracks, taking one small step at a time and making every effort to move in complete silence. I knew I was close to this deer. I had walked only about twenty yards and there, staring directly at me through the tag alders and the freshly falling snow, was a magnificent buck. He seemed to be confused, wondering how I had gotten that close to him without his hearing or smelling me. I slowly raised my rifle to my shoulder, took careful aim at the thickest part of his neck, and fired. He immediately whirled around and began running through the thick underbrush. I rushed over to where he had been standing and found blood and deer hair lying on top of the snow. I knew I had hit him, but I didn't know how badly he was injured.

I then did something I had never done before and have never done since. Normally, I would have waited for a bit before I began tracking a wounded deer so he would bed down, but in this case I worried that he was heading toward an area where hunters from another deer camp had their stands, so I started running after that deer. Although I was thirty-seven years old, the adrenaline must have been flowing, as I was leaping over windfalls and at a dead run with my rifle at port arms attempting to catch up with him. As soon as I got through the tag alders where the woods opened up into an area of large basswoods, I stopped and could see the buck standing broadside to me about a hundred yards away, trying to determine if I was still following him. I raised my rifle and emptied it in his direction, and he went down. I ran over to him and saw that he was a huge animal and had a perfect eight-point rack. I field dressed him, attached my deer tag, and returned to camp to summon help to get him back to the shack. Killing that magnificent buck became one of the highlights of my many years of deer hunting. I am still in disbelief that I was able to run after that deer, catch up with him, and deliver the fatal blow.

Winds of Change, 1982–1983

No one can explain why there are no entries in the shack log for the deer seasons of 1982 and 1983. My father wrote a note in the log, "Camp operated each season but nobody recorded '82 & '83. Shack damaged by falling trees 7/3/83 and in fall of '83 we did a lot of work cleaning roads, repairing shack and installing new roof. Three deer taken in 1983." The window shade that records deer kills shows that I shot a six-point buck and a doe in 1982 and that we shot two deer in 1983. Using my hunter's choice tag, I shot a doe, and Robin shot his first deer that year: a spike buck.

On July 3, 1983, straight-line winds tore through the area surrounding our hunting camp, changing the landscape and the way we would hunt for many years to come. The "golden land" of maples around the shack was gone forever and the road leading into the shack was clogged with downed trees. Local weather reports had estimated that the winds had been about eighty miles per hour, and it looked as if an atomic bomb had exploded in the area. Nothing was spared, and very few mature trees were left standing. We could no longer recognize the landmarks in the area, and we knew we had a huge task ahead of us just to cut our way in to the hunting shack to see if it had survived this devastating storm.

The weekend after the storm hit, we all gathered in force at the road and began to cut through the downed trees. All the regulars that hunted from our camp showed up for this event, armed

Devastation from the straight-line winds that had blown through the area in
the summer of 1983

with chainsaws and the goal of cutting a trail to the shack before
nightfall. It was hot, and the mosquitoes and deer flies were in
abundance. Cutting the debris off the road was no easy chore. The
wind had come from the west, and the first portion of the road
leading into the shack ran in a southerly direction, so all of the
trees had fallen fully across the road. The windstorm had been so
violent that the trees were intertwined; when they were cut, they
often acted as if they were spring-loaded, so that one had to be
extremely careful while cutting lest he be whacked with a branch.
It was a slow, tedious process, but by noon we were halfway there,
having cut a path just wide enough for the Coot to pass through.
After a short lunch break, we went back to the task at hand and
finally arrived at the shack late that afternoon.

We were all tired and wet with sweat but were completely
relieved to find that, although the entire area around the building
had been devastated, Blue Heaven and the three small outbuild-
ings had largely been spared. A large basswood next to the entry

door had broken off about midway down its thirty-foot trunk, and the top of the tree had clipped off a corner of the roof, but the other damage could be easily mitigated. For starters, the tree-top was still lying on the roof, which meant that it would be a challenge to slide it off without creating further damage, but we thought we could accomplish that. The chimney to the woodstove was also broken, but that could be replaced. So much debris had hit the shingles that it shattered the roofing, which would need replacement. Everything else was intact. All in all, we thought that it could have been much worse, as one of the fallen trees could have easily demolished any of the buildings. We returned to the shack on numerous weekends thereafter, building a ramp to slide the basswood off the shack roof, repairing the damages, and attempting to get the camp ready for the upcoming deer season.

When deer season 1983 arrived, we all knew that it would be a difficult hunt due to the thousands of trees that had been blown over in the area. We frequently spoke about staying at Blue Heaven at night but going out of the area during the day to hunt for deer. On opening morning, we all left camp and tried to reach our favorite hunting stands. It was almost impossible, as one had to climb over, crawl under, or find a way around all the trees that were blocking the normal routes to the hunting stands. We also questioned whether any deer were still in the area and believed that many of them might have gone elsewhere.

Robin was then sixteen years old and decided he would try to make his way down Birch Street to see if he could find any deer sign in the area. I was still at the shack loading my rifle to leave on the hunt when I heard him shoot numerous times. There was a pause, and then more gunfire. Another pause, and then a couple more shots. I started heading in his direction, figuring that he wasn't more than a couple hundred yards away from the shack. As I began crawling over, under, and on top of the fallen trees, I heard him yelling, "Dad! Dad! Dad!"

Fearing the worst, I moved toward him as quickly as possible and finally saw him standing in a hollow by a small creek. It appeared as if a deer was lying on the ground next to him. I finally reached him and asked what was wrong. I could see that the deer was mortally wounded but still alive. He responded, "I ran out of bullets!" He had shot a spike buck but had run out of ammunition before finishing the job. I quickly gave the deer a coup de grâce shot to put it out of its misery. Robin was thrilled to have shot his first buck.

We spent the remainder of the season trying to locate old landmarks and deer stands that were no longer recognizable due to all of the storm debris. I managed to shoot a doe later in the season near the shack, but no other deer were seen that year. We all felt as if we were trying to hunt in a foreign land.

A New Head Chef,
1984–1986

The next several years following the huge windstorm of 1983 would be spent trying to reclaim our hunting area around Blue Heaven. Whenever we went up to the shack during that time, we would have a work party and make an effort to cut open another trail to make it easier to reach one of our favorite deer stands. We knew that it was just a matter of time before loggers would come in to the area to harvest all of the downed timber, but until that time came, we had to depend on our own resources to make it possible to hunt near our deer camp.

My father wrote in the log on November 17, 1984:

Arrived Friday the 16th for deer season. All settled by 4 p.m. and Marv, John H., Bob H., J. K., Merle, Russ, Dennis and Adder in attendance. Merle killed 6 point buck 1st day but nothing else all season. We did not have any either-sex permits this year. Weather all season outstanding but hunting was poor. Woods are desolate due to the big blow of 7/3/83 but we all had a great time.

The log records in subsequent years reflect all the effort spent attempting to clear out the hunting grounds and return them to some degree of normalcy. If deer were in the area, they were difficult to see, and making a drive to push them anywhere was still out of the question. In 1985, heavy snow complicated the deer season, and we only shot one doe even though we had several hunter's choice permits.

The spring of 1986 presented quite a scare to the Jolly Boys. The county was moving to possibly eliminate the Recreational Use Permits for deer camps, and the county board held a large meeting to invite public input. At that time, only two other counties in Wisconsin were still granting the permits. Both my father and Adder attended the meeting, along with a multitude of others who held the permits for deer camps. The *Sawyer County Record* newspaper quoted my father as addressing the county board and stating, "I have gone to hunting camps since I was a kid and we have a tradition. My son killed his first buck at our camp and his son did too. We searched for wild land to buy to build our deer camp and believe me, there isn't much available." He also argued that the county needed to promote hunting in the area, and the camp permits made that possible. Adder also addressed the county board, saying, "We think it's a great privilege to have this right for a camp on county property and to be able to hunt on it. We don't complain about the fee."

The fee for the Recreational Use Permit at that time was only fifty dollars per year. Shortly after this meeting, the fee was raised to one hundred dollars per year, which was still a bargain in the eyes of the Jolly Boys. They had been hunting on this area of county property for more than thirty years and didn't want to have to move their camp off county land. Ultimately, the county board decided to extend the Recreational Use Permits to the present permit holders, but also wanted to start a twenty-five-year phase-out of the permits, as other neighboring counties had done. This issue of terminating the Recreational Use Permits would continue to be a topic of discussion in the years to come.

That deer season, my younger son, Oliver, came to deer camp. He had turned fourteen and was now allowed to come up to hunt

My youngest son, Ollie, started hunting in 1986 at age fourteen and hasn't missed a deer season since.

with the Jolly Boys. Ollie had been eagerly anticipating his opportunity to be up at the shack with his grandpa, dad, and brother and spent that entire season tramping every square inch of the woods looking for deer. Although he did not find success his first year at the shack, there was no doubt in anyone's mind about his enthusiasm for the hunt.

Hunting conditions improved slightly in 1986 and 1987, and we were able to harvest three deer in each of those two seasons. We also saw more deer sign in the area. Saplings were springing up in the blown-down tree debris, giving the deer more food and shelter. But other signs of change weren't so positive. My father entered his seventies, and it became obvious that standing next to that old wood cookstove preparing the meals at camp was taking its toll on him. The time had come for him to kick back and sit at the table, play cribbage, and allow someone else to do the grunt work of cooking. He had been the head chef at Blue Heaven from the start. Merle would help out on occasion, but my father had always done the planning, the grocery shopping, and the cooking for our group. Late one afternoon at the shack I could see he was visibly tired. I told him that it was time for him to step down and that I would take over for him. He didn't argue.

My father excelled at cooking almost all of the menu items at camp. One exception was fried eggs, which the hunters in our camp called "snotty eggs." He always fried the eggs in gobs of butter in the huge cast-iron skillet that we also used for frying venison. He served the eggs directly from the skillet to the plates on the table sitting in front of the hunters. He would grab an egg or two with the spatula and then ask the hunter, "How do you want your eggs?" No one ever responded, because the eggs were always cooked the same way, slightly singed on the bottom and totally undercooked on the top.

My first priority as new head chef was to serve properly cooked fried eggs. To accomplish that task, I purchased a large nonstick frypan and brought it up to the shack. I put in a small pat of butter, allowed it to melt, got the pan hot, and cracked the eggs into the pan. I then added about a tablespoon of water to the pan and put a tight lid on it so the tops of the eggs would steam while they were frying on medium heat. The eggs always turned out perfectly cooked. The whites of the eggs were cooked through, and the yolks were always creamy and ready to be broken with a piece of toast. Everyone was thrilled to finally get properly cooked eggs, and although a few joked that they missed my dad's "snotty eggs," we always knew that they were kidding.

RIBS AND KRAUT

My father was aware that I knew my way around the kitchen. My mother taught me how to cook in my early teens when both of my parents were working late hours in their grocery store. My sister didn't like to cook, so my mother would call me from work, inform me of the menu for the evening meal, and then guide me through the preparation step by step. I was soon making chicken, pot roast, and similar dinners with ease.

At Blue Heaven, we have a number of favorites that we dine on during the first weekend of deer camp. Second only to the Reali spaghetti, pork ribs with sauerkraut is requested by everyone each year. Properly prepared, it is probably the best of comfort foods. Improperly prepared, it can be disastrous, even painful.

My father served ribs and kraut the first Saturday night on the opening weekend every year at Blue Heaven beginning in the early sixties. He would purchase pork ribs and sauerkraut, place everything in a roasting pan with a tight lid on it, and allow it to slow cook in the oven of the wood-burning cookstove for about three hours, until the meat was falling off the bone. He used what he lovingly referred to as his "rotation method." This involved pulling the roaster out of the oven about every half hour or so, rotating the roaster 180 degrees so all the ingredients would turn upside down, and then sliding it back into the oven for further cooking. The ribs always turned out delicious and were served over buttered baked potatoes with generous amounts of salt and pepper. Everyone always raved, and enormous quantities were consumed by the hungry hunters.

There was just one minor problem. Most of the hunters in the camp ended up with various degrees of lower intestinal distress shortly after dinner. The outhouse would be in constant demand throughout the evening and the early morning hours. It didn't take a rocket scientist to figure out that consuming the grease from the pork ribs and the brine from the sauerkraut might not be a good thing for the body. It had the same effect as a strong laxative.

After a number of years of this abuse, I pleaded with my father to allow me to cook the ribs and kraut. After much debate, he finally gave in and let me try my skill at preparing this popular dish. First, I rendered the fat off the ribs by precooking them in the oven until they turned brown. This eliminated much of that nasty fat within the meat. I also purchased the sauerkraut in plastic bags rather than in cans or jars. This way I could snip the top of the bag and squeeze out the majority of the brine from the sauerkraut before cooking. I then took things one step further and fried the kraut in a frypan with a little butter to steam off any remaining brine. I put the ribs in a large roasting pan with the sauerkraut on top of the ribs, and covered the roasting pan with a tight layer of aluminum foil to seal in all the juices while everything slow-roasted. Amazingly enough, my method of cooking this dish equaled my father's, with one exception: no one got sick. You will love this recipe.

Ingredients

1 pound pork ribs or country-style pork ribs per person (for the best flavor, buy ribs that are meaty but not overly lean)

1 (32-ounce) plastic bag of sauerkraut for every three people

Salt and pepper

3 tablespoons butter or margarine

1 large russet baking potato per person

Preparation

Cut the pork ribs into serving portions, about three to four inches wide. If you're using country-style ribs, there is no need to do anything. Place the pork on a broiling pan and liberally salt and pepper both sides of the pork. Put the pork into a 400-degree oven or under the broiler, and bake or broil both sides of the pork until they start to turn brown but do not overcook. This will take about one half an hour. Discard fat and put the pork into a deep roasting pan.

Snip the tops of the sauerkraut bags and squeeze the kraut to remove the brine. Remove the sauerkraut from the bags and put it into a nonstick frypan with about three tablespoons of butter. Slowly fry the sauerkraut on medium heat until it starts to brown; do not overcook. Remove the sauerkraut from the pan and place it on top of the ribs.

Cover the top of the roaster with aluminum foil to make an airtight seal. Preheat oven to 325 degrees and cook for two and a half to three hours until the top of the sauerkraut is a golden brown and the ribs fall apart with the touch of a fork.

Serve with baked potatoes. The potatoes can be baked while the ribs and kraut are baking. Cut potatoes open and butter them heavily, adding salt and pepper to taste. This meal is best served with the sauerkraut on top of the baked potato and the ribs to the side.

SHACK GREEN BEANS
WITH VINEGAR, ONION, AND BACON

In late February of 1987, my parents, Dennis, Ollie, and I went up to the shack on a Saturday night just to relax, play some cards, and have a good venison dinner. There was enough snow on the ground for snowmobiling, and we had just settled in when we saw two snowmobilers coming up the trail toward the shack. They stopped and removed their helmets. It was Chuck and his daughter Stephanie from Nelson Lake Landing. My parents knew them well, as they would often stop at Chuck's resort for a hamburger and pitcher of beer. Chuck's wife, Linda, was in California visiting her parents, and my father immediately extended an invitation for Chuck and his daughter to join us for a venison fry that evening. Chuck readily accepted, but only on the condition that they could contribute to the dinner. Unbeknownst to us, Chuck gathered wild mushrooms every fall, and he insisted that I go over to the resort and bring back several packages he had in his freezer to go with the venison steak. Our dinner that evening was one to remember. Fried venison tenderloins with Chuck's sautéed wild mushrooms, Shack Baked Potatoes, and a shack dish my dad had invented called Shack Green Beans. Shack Green Beans complement a variety of main dishes and have somewhat of a German flair to them as they are cooked with vinegar, onion, and bacon.

Ingredients

1 pound bacon
1 onion, chopped into large pieces
3 (14.5-ounce) cans cut green beans
2 cups red wine vinegar
Salt and pepper

Preparation

This dish is very simple to put together and will serve 6 to 8 people. Take one pound of bacon, slice it into one-inch cubes, and fry it in a large frypan until it is very crispy. Remove the bacon pieces from the bacon fat and place on a paper towel to drain. Using the bacon grease in the pan, sauté the onion until tender and transparent. Drain the bacon grease off the onion. Drain the green beans and put in the pan with the onion. Add the bacon and vinegar. Liberally salt and pepper and simmer everything for about an hour or until all of the vinegar evaporates.

A Successful Season,
1987–1989

The decade of the 1980s wound down without much excitement or fanfare up at the hunting shack. In 1987, Dennis shot a very nice eight-point buck, and I shot a small buck and a doe. We had three either-sex permits that year, and two of them went unfilled. The following year we also had three either-sex permits, and filled none of them. We almost got skunked until I managed to shoot a small four-pointer, but by that time it was too late in the season to cut up the deer for our table. We were without venison but still ate well. We dined on meatloaf on the first Friday night, followed by spaghetti for Saturday, and a wonderful pork roast with all of the trimmings on Sunday. Monday night we settled for leftover spaghetti, and on Tuesday we dined on the leftover pork roast. It was almost embarrassing that we were at deer camp and didn't have venison to enjoy, but we made it through the remainder of the season savoring ribs and kraut and a pot roast cooked to perfection with potatoes and carrots. We also had lots of leftover turkey from Thanksgiving, so we made do without venison that year.

In the fall of 1989, we organized a work party to finish cutting a trail through the storm debris of 1983 up to the Can on North Lane. Even though it had been six years since the straight-line winds, much of our hunting area remained a mess. With the completion of this project, we finally felt as if we had reclaimed most of our hunting area.

Deer season 1989 turned out to be very successful. A couple of inches of snow covered the ground, and we had five hunter's choice permits between the eight of us in camp. We had an open bunk, and I had received permission from the Jolly Boys to invite a friend by the name of Randy Stuggen up from Milwaukee for the opening weekend. My dad, Adder, Russ, and Uncle Bobby were getting up there in age, so Dennis and I welcomed a younger hunter to join the two of us in pushing the deer around. Although we saw lots of deer tracks and sign in the area on opening day, no one saw any deer.

Sunday was much better. I found a place to sit early that morning on a stand we named the Ravine, which is high on a hill in the hardwoods overlooking a tag alder swamp. I settled in and felt optimistic that a deer would be walking along the edge of that swamp at any moment. I had been sitting there for about fifteen minutes and was starting to do some serious daydreaming when a deer stood up from behind a windfall about a hundred yards away. The deer apparently hadn't heard me walking into my stand but had gotten a smell of me once I settled in. He didn't see me, but I saw him. I put my scope on the deer and could see it was a spike buck. One shot, and the deer went down in the bed from which he had risen. At noon on that day, Dennis connected with an eight-point buck several hundred yards north of where I had been sitting that morning. Dennis got turned around after he dressed the deer and headed back to camp, and we had a tough time finding the deer later that afternoon. We had an even more difficult time dragging the deer through several swamps to get to a location where we could transport it back to the shack using the Coot. We had two bucks hanging, and everyone was chomping at the bit to return to the woods the next morning for more action.

Monday turned out to be even more exciting than Sunday. I was walking on a deer trail next to the swamp toward the Big Rock when a herd of deer came running directly at me: two bucks and

three does. My attention went first to the biggest buck, which
had a five-point rack. I dropped him after two shots. I then fired
three shots at the smaller buck that had eight-inch spike antlers,
and he went down. I immediately changed clips in my rifle and
started shooting at the does that were running up a hill away from
all the commotion. I managed to get one, but the other two made
their escape. A few moments later, both Randy and my Uncle
Bob, who had heard all of the shots, showed up at my location.
Randy had never dressed a deer before, so I was able to teach him;
he then took over and dressed out the other two deer. My uncle
had already started back to the shack to summon transportation
and to spread the news that I had three deer lying in the woods.

　　We took it easy for the remainder of that deer season. When it
came time to break camp, we had five deer hanging from the deer
pole and felt we had plenty of venison to share with everyone. The
1989 season had been great for Wisconsin deer hunters. There had
been 661,713 licenses sold and 310,192 deer registered.

Butchering the Deer

Butchering a deer is very much like the art of properly field-dressing a deer. It's not something that one does every day. The first time one is called upon to do it, the technique feels very foreign. The second time is easier, as one knows what to expect. Like everything else, the more times one is exposed to dressing out a deer or cutting it up, the more proficient one becomes, and eventually the whole process becomes second nature.

In the early years at Blue Heaven, cutting up the venison was relatively simple, as there weren't many deer in the area and not many deer were taken during the deer season. More often than not, the Jolly Boys only shot one or two deer over the course of the entire season, and those deer were skinned and cut up to eat while the hunters were still up at deer camp. In the years that followed, when deer became more plentiful and more than one or two deer were harvested, plans had to be made to butcher the animals after deer season.

My father was a very skilled butcher. Everyone who watched him cut up meat thought he had the skills of an experienced surgeon. He had been in the grocery business for the majority of his life and spent a considerable amount of time behind the meat counter. There was little he didn't know about meat and how to cut it up properly. He had the various butchering tools to prove it, with a vast collection of Chicago Cutlery that he had accumulated over the years. He kept all of his knives in a special cloth carrying case and they were always razor sharp. Merle and Russ Clagett also knew how to cut up a deer, having learned the skill from others during their many years of deer hunting.

It was a tedious chore to butcher the deer once the season had ended. The deer were taken to my father's garage and hung from the rafters. The hunters selected a day to meet at my parents' house to tackle the chore, usually in very cold weather, and usually the deer were completely frozen. The hunters would go to the garage with their knives and skin the frozen hides off the deer, cutting the deer into sections to be brought into the house for further processing. By the time they completed this task, everyone had stiff hands from working in the cold. We all chipped in to accomplish the various tasks, and each person had a job to do dependent on his individual skill level. Some would be involved in "boning out" the meat, which is removing the meat from the bones. Others would use knives to remove the tallow from the meat, and to make sure that the meat was as free of hair and tallow as possible. We used lots of damp paper towels in the process of removing stray deer hair, and we sorted the meat into piles for steaks, stew meat, hamburger, and roasts. The project would usually start midafternoon on the selected day, and it would be late in the evening before everything had been cut up, wrapped, and labeled. We would then equally divide the meat among the hunters, except for the coveted sirloins and tenderloins, which we reserved for special Jolly Boys events. My mother's kitchen ended up in a complete mess during this process, but she never complained.

As the years passed and deer became more plentiful, cutting up the meat became too much of a chore to accomplish in my parents' kitchen. The Jolly Boys decided that it made sense to butcher the deer up at Blue Heaven during the final weekend of the deer season. The deer we had harvested were taken to town, registered with the DNR, and then brought back to camp for butchering. With all of the skill and manpower we had at hand, no one ever gave a thought to taking the deer to a butcher shop for processing, nor did the Jolly Boys ever consider turning the venison into sausage, brats, or beer sticks. They enjoyed the natural flavor of venison too much.

On the last Friday of the season, we brought the deer inside the shack and hung them from the rafters so they would thaw overnight. We laid a plastic tarp on the floor to catch any loose hair or blood from the thawing animals. After an early breakfast the next morning, we would begin removing the deer hides in the warmth of the hunting shack so they could be butchered. I'm certain that my mother was overjoyed that we would no longer be making a mess out of her kitchen. Moreover, butchering the deer while at deer camp was the perfect way to pass deer-butchering skills from father to son.

Once we removed the deer hides, the deer carcasses were ready to be cut into sections and taken outside to be kept cool. We always hung the deer by their hind legs to facilitate the skinning and butchering. Once we skinned them, we used a meat saw to remove the head, along with the attached deer hide. Then we cut the neck off to be turned into a neck roast or boned out for stew or hamburger meat. We cut the front shoulders off next, to be saved for roasts or boned out for stew or hamburger meat. It then took three men to separate the main body of the deer from the hindquarters. Two men had to hold the heavy torso while a third man cut and sawed until it detached from the hindquarters. Finally, we cut the two hindquarters each into two sections.

Once the deer were skinned and sectioned, we cleaned up any mess that we'd made and prepared for the process of cutting and wrapping all of the venison. The large lumberjack table on which we dined served as our butcher block, with a multitude of cutting boards lying on the table. Almost everyone at our camp had his

Russ Clagett uses his favorite boning knife to carefully remove the sirloins from the upper portion of the spine.

own favorite set of knives that he used for boning out and cutting up the meat. We started by bringing in the main body section of the deer, which contains the ribs and sirloins. The sirloins, which many refer to as back straps, run along the top back spine of the deer. The tenderloins run along the underside of the spine. Usually, we would have already removed the tenderloins right after the deer was killed. This is because they are easily accessible once the deer has been field dressed, and if they aren't removed right away, they will dry out and this coveted piece of meat won't be much good. We cut away any salvageable meat left on the main section and put it in a pile to be ground into hamburger, which is excellent in both chili and spaghetti recipes.

The Jolly Boys never did anything with the venison ribs, as they contained too much strong tallow. We usually discarded them and put them out for the chickadees to enjoy. We wrapped the loins whole in freezer paper, to be cut into steaks at a future time, just before being flash-fried at a special event. We then brought the front shoulders in, cleaned them up, and cut them into roasts. A considerable amount of time was spent cleaning up the hindquarters, and as much round steak would be cut from them as possible. We threw any scraps in a bucket for stew meat or grinding into hamburger. Depending on how many deer had to be butchered, it usually took the entire morning and afternoon before everything was wrapped in freezer paper and labeled. Nothing went to waste. We coveted the venison too much for that to happen. Even the deer hides were taken to town and sold to be made into gloves and clothing. When the Jolly Boys finished butchering a deer, the only things left were the deer hooves, and even those were often given away to someone who had a use for them.

Pratfalls, 1990

An entry in the shack log, dated October 20, 1990, reads in part:

> Work party consisting of Marv, John, Robin, Russ, Dennis
> & Bob arrive to open camp & prepare for deer season. Split
> wood & cut more yellow birch for next season. Russell had
> volunteered to bring venison tenderloins for supper, but the
> package turned out to be a large venison shank roast! Made
> do with making Shack Steak out of the shank roast and added
> some hamburger to it and served it over mashed potatoes.

Lesson learned: Always properly label your wrapped meat before throwing it into the freezer. Needless to say, Russ ended up taking quite a bit of ribbing from the rest of us for several years following that incident.

Deer season 1990 was nearly a bust, but we still had a lot of fun. We had seven hunter's choice permits between us and all nine bunks were full, but the weather wasn't cooperating. There was no snow, and record highs were being registered with temperatures rising into the high sixties each day. On opening morning Rob managed to shoot a doe, but the rest of the deer tags went unfilled that season. It was impossible to locate the deer in the area without any snow on the ground.

The highlights of that season came in the form of humor. Russ related that he had been hunting when "nature called" and, like most hunters, he simply dropped his pants and took care of his business. He redressed, began to continue on his hunt, and then fell flat on his face. It appears that when he pulled his hunting pants back up, he neglected to pull up his long johns, so they got tangled around his ankles, causing him to trip. He was happy no one had been around to witness the event. Not to be outdone, my father reported that he had been walking down a hill and slipped on some leaves. He fell to the ground and couldn't get back up on his feet no matter how hard he shoved himself up with his hand. It turned out that my dad had been trying to shove himself up with the hand he had on top of his "heater-seater," which he had clipped to the back of the belt on his pants. He was also happy no one had been around to witness the event.

Adder's Ladder

After Adder turned seventy-nine, we all noticed that he was having difficulty getting in and out of his bunk, which was in the center between my father's and Merle's. Although a chair was placed there to be used as a stepping stool, Adder was not a tall man, and his bunk was almost five feet off the floor. It was difficult for a man his age to maneuver in and out of that center bunk, and we all knew that he would not be comfortable in a lower bunk where it got too cold during the night. We were concerned that he might hurt himself in the middle of the night if he tried to get out of his bunk.

I looked around in my garage at home, found some scrap two-by-twelves, and constructed Adder a twelve-inch-wide stairway to reach from the floor to the top of his bunk. I took a black marker, wrote "Adder's Ladder" on it, and brought the stairway up with me for the 1990 deer season.

I must admit that I had some misgivings about presenting that ladder as a gift to Adder. I certainly didn't want to insult him. On the first day at camp, I slid the stairway into the shack and laid it on the floor, explaining its function to Adder. To my delight, he was thrilled. We immediately installed it next to his bunk, and he used it to get into and out of his bunk for several years. He even brought up pieces of scrap carpeting to install on the steps to prevent the possibility of getting splinters in his bare feet.

"Snowdin," 1991

The hunters at Blue Heaven often speculated that it would be a thrill to be snowed in at the hunting shack during deer season. We figured it would be great fun to be stranded deep in the woods with ample food and drink, riding out a major winter storm, with no place to go and nothing to do except deal the cards! As the old saying goes, "Be careful what you wish for."

The autumn of 1991 had been beautiful. We spent several weekends preparing the hunting camp for the upcoming deer season scheduled to begin on November 23. On October 31, a major winter storm cranked up and swept through northwestern Wisconsin, depositing up to thirty inches of heavy, wet snow. Sixteen inches fell in the Hayward area, and there were many reports of old structures collapsing under the heavy weight of the snow. The event became known as "The Halloween Storm of 1991." We were excited to see the early snowfall, as it assured good hunting conditions for the entire deer season.

We arrived at camp on Friday, November 22, to find the forest floor covered in wet snow. The woods were full of water, as it had rained for several days following the Halloween Storm. On the first Saturday of the season, we awoke to several inches of new snow. It was rough going in the woods, but we managed to get three deer on the opening weekend. Dennis shot a small buck on the following Tuesday, and the next day we received an additional six inches of snow. I found myself struggling to walk through the heavy snow in the woods, troubled by a hernia I had gotten by lifting up and draining a boat filled with rainwater that previous summer. I was delaying having surgery for the hernia repair until after deer season, as I didn't want to be recovering from the surgery while at deer camp.

Several of us remained in camp for Thanksgiving Day and were joined by our other family members for a celebration. The following day, Friday, marked the start of the last weekend of deer season. No new snow had fallen, but there was already an ample amount on the ground and the weather was too cold for any of it to melt.

We had numerous either-sex permits that year, and Ollie shot three deer from his tree stand just as it began to snow very heavily about 3:30 p.m. on Friday. By 5 p.m., we knew we were in for some very nasty winter weather. As the evening progressed, Dennis grew increasingly concerned about our safety if we got snowed in. In particular, he was worried about the older Jolly Boys. What if they developed a medical condition? How would we get them out? Would the snow load collapse the roof of our thirty-five-year-old hunting shack? How would we get the Coot back out to the road? How would we be able to transport the seven deer hanging on the buck pole along with all of the gear everyone had? How would I be able to make it back out to the road with my hernia, walking in waist-deep snow? Dennis was a mess and on the verge of hyperventilating. He needed to take action. About 2 a.m. on Saturday, he left his bunk and woke up my son Rob to assist him in firing up the Coot. The two of them decided to try to bust a trail to the highway and keep the road open. About twelve inches of snow had already fallen, and the Coot didn't operate well in the snow. Although the two of them made several trips back and forth between the shack and the highway where our cars were parked, they finally abandoned their efforts just as dawn broke.

There was simply too much snow. Seventeen inches of new snow had fallen overnight to add to what was already on the ground. ~~Everyone woke up early that morning and we developed an es-~~ cape plan while having our morning coffee. Rob and Ollie would walk out to the highway and dig out a vehicle. They would then go to town to get Ollie's snowmobile for transportation and my dad's snowblower to blow out a path to get our vehicles dug out. The rest of us would stay at camp and cut up the seven deer we had harvested that deer season. We would then play poker until they returned to rescue us.

We spent the day skinning out and cutting up the seven deer, and by midafternoon Rob and Ollie came ramming through the woods on Ollie's snowmobile. There was jubilation—we had been rescued! They brought good news. Adder, who had been unable to join us for the final weekend of deer camp, knew we were snowbound and in trouble. He had sent my cousin up with his pickup and plow to clear a path through the snow so we could drive out onto the highway. We were feeling some relief. The cards were dealt, and we all enjoyed a final Saturday evening in the hunting camp surrounded by a winter wonderland.

On Sunday morning, the trek from the shack to the main highway began, and it was quite a project. Ollie had driven his snowmobile back and forth between the shack and the highway numerous times to create a trail and pack the snow down, but we still had to get the Coot out to the highway. We loaded it with our gear and the venison. We then hooked the snowmobile to the front of the Coot, and everyone assisted in shoving the Coot and the snowmobile down the trail as the snowmobile struggled and smoked, trying to pull the Coot to the highway.

After a morning of hard work, we were successful, and everyone was able to get his vehicle out onto the highway. Everyone except for Bobby, that is, whose old beat-up Buick was still stuck in the snow. He lovingly referred to that old wreck as his "deer-hunting car." I attached a tow strap to his rear bumper, and we tried to pull it free with a four-wheel-drive Jeep, but the bumper of that old rusty Buick ripped off and went flying through the snow. Bobby was upset over the damage to his car but took it in stride. We shoveled his vehicle out by hand and loaded his bumper into his backseat. He left all of us standing there chuckling as he left for Superior.

A few weeks later I had my planned hernia surgery. While I was recovering at home, I became inspired to write a poem to send to everyone to record the event of getting snowed in.

'Twas the last Friday, season's end was drawing near;
Snowflakes started falling, we were running low on beer.
Ollie had just killed three, the time was almost four;
Getting dark and nasty, snow on forest floor.
Seven deer had been taken, one was quite small;
No problem there, 'twas better than none at all.
Dennis looked worried, concerned about the weather;
Pacing back and forth, working up such a tether.
"John's got a hernia! Marvin's getting old,
How the heck we getting back out to the road?"
"The Coot won't make it, the snow's really thick!
Anyone in the outhouse? I think I have to ****!"
John said, "Chill out, Dennis, we've got plenty to eat,
Somehow we'll make it, let's take care of the meat.
Haul 'em in the shack, hang them by upper bunk;
Stoke up the fires, we'll drink and get drunk.
Forget about the weather, we'll cut them up at dawn;
All the big deer, and Russ' buck fawn."
The cards were dealt, but Dennis really got nervous;
He threw on his boots, "Let's put the Coot into service!"
Snow kept on falling, as the Coot left the shack;
Dennis at the wheel, and Rob shovin' in the back.

One hour later, two snowmen did appear;
Dennis totally white, and Rob still pushing in the rear.
~~All through the night, Dennis laid in his bed;~~
With visions of tragedy dancing through his head.
Up every two hours, to bust a trail to the road;
Almost a useless effort, wasted in the cold.
Dawn finally came, seventeen inches had fallen;
The old army commo phone bell dinged twice,
     who could be callin'?
It was Peter with Adder, wondering of our plight;
Were we stranded and okay? Had we made it through
     the night?
Adder wanted to come in, but there was no place to park;
We told him to forget it, he couldn't disembark.
Rob and Ollie left for town, marching waist deep in snow;
Rob's Jeep wouldn't start, and he had to locate a tow.
The boys were on a mission, Ollie's snowmobile we
     would need;
The Coot no longer would make it, to this we would concede.
Several hours later, came a-crashing down the trail;
Two smiling Hanson kids, their mission did not fail.
We had been rescued, the meat was finally cut;
On with the game, forget about the "rut!"
The phone dinged again, 'twas Craig Hanson on the line;
Adder had sent him, and he plowed us out in time.
The crisis almost over, Dennis began to feel great;
Took paper sack off his head, no longer would he
     hyperventilate.
The hunters were at peace now, and enjoyed their
     Saturday night;
Sunday would be a breeze, after experiencing such a fright.
The exodus went smoothly, as we trailered out our gear;
Sunday at ten, we finally ran out of beer.

The last task before us was to pull out the Coot;
Dennis said, "Leave it till summer, I really don't give a hoot."
We tied Ollie's snowmobile with a strap to the Coot's front;
Several started pushing, did they ever groan and grunt.
It was quite an ordeal, but somehow we got out;
It wasn't very easy, but accomplished with muscle and clout.
The last task at hand, pull Bobby's car from the snow;
Just hook up the tow strap, and away he would go.
The tow strap was connected, between the two cars;
It was stretched and tied, between rear face-bars.
Russ' Jeep pulled and tightened, the long nylon strap;
The next thing we heard, was a soft breaking crack.
There lay Bobby's bumper, away it did go;
Flying from his Buick, and sliding through the snow.
All we could hear, was a voice from afar;
What the **** have you guys done, to my deer hunting car?!?!

Soon after the deer season of 1991, Ollie showed up sporting a new customized license plate on the back of his four-wheel-drive pickup truck that stated, "SNOWDIN."

More Snow, 1992–1993

The winter of 1992 was another banner year for snow. The shack log has multiple entries by many of us who snowmobiled or cross-country skied in to Blue Heaven to keep the roof shoveled and have a weekend party or two. The following fall, it was once again time to level the shack and cut wood for the upcoming deer season. The shack had been built on wood and concrete block piers without any footings, and each spring it would become unleveled because of the heavy clay soil, which caused several of the piers to either sink or rise with the spring thaw. It was a constant battle but a chore that had to be undertaken or else the doors and windows wouldn't function properly. We had to crawl under the shack, which sat only about a foot off the ground, and raise or lower certain areas with hydraulic jacks in our attempt to level it. My mother often quipped that we had the only self-cleaning table she had ever seen, because if someone accidently spilled a drink on it, the liquid would quickly run off the tabletop and onto the floor.

There were eight of us in attendance for that deer season. Although the deer in Wisconsin were reported as being plentiful, we saw very little deer sign in our area. The only deer we shot was a six-point buck, even though we possessed several hunter's choice and bonus-deer permits. Ollie finally grew impatient and went north to hunt with some friends in the Eau Claire Lakes area, bringing back a doe for camp meat. After the season ended, the reports stated that the deer harvest in our area was down 50 percent from the previous year.

Merle didn't attend deer camp with us that year. He was beginning to spend less and less time up at the shack during deer season, choosing instead to go to another deer camp north of us with Adder's oldest son, Peter. Peter loved to hunt but had multiple allergies. One of those allergies was smoke from cigars and cigarettes, and the other was deer hair. Adder's youngest son, Philip, had married a woman who also liked to hunt, so Philip opted to hunt with her and her family in the Phillips, Wisconsin, area. We knew Merle still loved Blue Heaven, but he frequently felt more relaxed hunting at a camp with only two or three other hunters and where things were more peaceful.

The following year provided no either-sex permits for hunters in our area during the deer season. Due to the low deer herd, the season was buck-only, and we all speculated that the heavy snows of the 1991–1992 winter had taken their toll on the deer and fawn population. We had very little snow on the ground for the 1993 season until Thanksgiving Day, when we finally received five inches of new snow. We hunted hard for the last weekend of the season, but we observed no deer and very few deer tracks. It was a disappointing season because we didn't get any venison for our table, but we all still thoroughly enjoyed Blue Heaven.

One person who wasn't having such a good time was Adder. He was beginning to show his eighty-three years that season. He no longer had any desire to leave the shack to hunt, but would instead stay behind doing a few odd kitchen chores, sitting at the table reading, or taking frequent naps. He had developed a sleep problem. He would pace around the shack in the dead of night when the rest of us were in our bunks and end up in his bunk for most of the daylight hours. We finally took him into town to his doctor to see if something could be done to correct his sleep patterns.

Changing of the Guard

During the deer season of 1993, several things were put into motion that would change Blue Heaven for many years to come. The hunting camp was then almost forty years old, and only three of the original Jolly Boys remained: my father, Adder, and Merle. It became obvious to Dennis and me that it was increasingly difficult for the three of them to handle all of the responsibilities of shack ownership. Adder was in his eighties and had developed sleeping issues, my father was in his midseventies, and Merle wasn't far behind, showing less and less interest in coming to Blue Heaven for deer season. Although my father was still very active in our camp, he was no longer able to gather all of the supplies and handle cooking chores. None of the original Jolly Boys were able to perform much maintenance to the shack, due to their age. Dennis and I were becoming concerned about the future of the hunting camp and wanted to take action to preserve the tradition.

Dennis and his father had been regular members of the hunting camp for almost twenty-five years, and we all considered them honorary Jolly Boys. Dennis and I decided that we would attempt to purchase the hunting camp from the Jolly Boys to assure that the two of us, his father, and my two sons would always have Blue Heaven.

Toward the end of the deer season, I approached my father with the idea that Dennis and I would purchase the camp. My father was well aware that the original Jolly Boys' agreement stated that no one Jolly Boy could sell his share in the camp. According to the agreement, if a Jolly Boy left or died, his share would pass to the survivors. However, he also knew that I was trying to enable things to remain the same as each of the three remaining Jolly Boys passed away or could no longer be there to hunt. He also felt strongly that someday the camp should be in the hands of his grandsons, as they were the logical future owners.

We all knew that the hunting shack wasn't worth much money. The building was showing a great deal of wear and tear and the contents within had outlived their useful lives quite some time ago. The hunting camp was situated on land leased to the Jolly Boys by the county; therefore, only real property would be involved in the sale. There was no real estate, but Dennis and I were fine with that. We knew that we'd only be purchasing tradition and a lot of memories, but we'd be making certain that Blue Heaven would continue to thrive even after the original Jolly Boys were no longer around. I knew that in order to convince Adder and Merle to sell, they would need assurances that they wouldn't be excluded for so long as they both were alive and wanted to come to the shack. I therefore drafted a purchase agreement to present to them and my father.

The purpose of the agreement was to supersede any previous agreements that had been made by the five original Jolly Boys regarding the hunting camp. The agreement spelled out that, although ownership of the camp and the responsibilities of operating the camp would be transferred to Dennis and me, the Jolly Boys would be granted all of the privileges that they previously enjoyed and would retain the rights to their assigned bunks and lockers for so long as they desired. We also assured the Jolly Boys that all of the established rules would continue unchanged to assure that the camp continued to perpetuate.

~~It wasn't difficult to convince the Jolly Boys to sell the camp.~~ They all felt that the burden of maintaining the camp needed to be passed on and that it was time for someone else to manage the finances and take care of the insurance, taxes, and camp permit. We easily agreed on a purchase price, and in January of 1994, Dennis and I became the owners of Blue Heaven. The Recreational Use Permit was transferred into our names. It was a win-win situation, and Dennis and I believed that we were capable of continuing the tradition of the Jolly Boys and Blue Heaven for years to come.

Loss, 1994

We had a devastating discovery at the shack when we arrived for the annual spring frolic and work party on Friday, April 15, 1994. Sometime after the deer season in 1993, someone had broken into the shack and made a mess of the place.

The weather that April weekend was horrible. The temperature was in the lower forties with a strong wind, abundant rain, and heavy snow showers. The road into the shack was full of water. Ollie had buried his new pickup in a mud hole as he attempted to drive in with the supplies. We arrived on foot, cold and wet, to find that the glass of the two doors had been broken and the vandals had also broken one of the large windows. Glass was everywhere, but nothing appeared to be missing. We spent the rest of the evening hauling our supplies in by hand and attempting to secure the shack for the night by putting plastic over the broken doors and window. We weren't able to eat our supper until 11 p.m., and it took until midnight to finally get the shack warm and comfortable enough to retire for the night.

The next day dawned clear and mild, but it was still very windy. We spent the morning digging the pickup out of the mud and then made a trip into town to purchase replacement glass to repair the doors and windows. Several men stayed at camp to finish cleaning up the debris and to wash all the dishes and everything else that had been exposed to the elements for several months. By Saturday night, things had pretty much returned to normal, but we left the shack on Sunday afternoon concerned by the possibility of future break-ins and vandalism. Several inspection trips were made into the shack over the course of that summer. To our relief, we discovered no further vandalism.

Still, the potential for burglary and vandalism to our hunting shack had always concerned us. The place sits unoccupied for months at a time, and it is deep in the woods, far off the beaten path. It's a risk that we've had to accept. We consider ourselves fortunate that, for the most part, people who pass by our camp respect the fact that it is property belonging to others, and their curiosity to see what's inside vanishes as they pass by.

But the vandalism of the spring was nothing compared to the loss we suffered that summer. In August 1994, my dad—the best of the Jolly Boys, in my opinion—died. His heart stopped suddenly. Although they helicoptered him to Eau Claire, where valiant efforts were made to revive him, his doctors informed us that there was nothing that could be done, and we ultimately made the decision to have all his life-support systems removed. His passing had a profound and lasting impact on Blue Heaven. His skill at organizing the trips to the shack would be greatly missed and difficult to replace. We all knew there would be a massive void at deer season and the other events held at Blue Heaven in the following years.

When deer season 1994 arrived, we knew things at Blue Heaven would be very different from past years. My dad's passing earlier that year was still weighing heavily on all of us and due to his advanced age, Adder declined to join us for the hunt. Merle was fighting a virus and wasn't feeling well, and he advised us that he wouldn't be in attendance opening weekend either. For the first time ever, there would be no Jolly Boys in camp on opening day.

Marv and Violet prove that happiness is a perfectly cooked prime rib roast from the woodstove oven at Blue Heaven.

Seven hunters arrived at the shack for opening weekend. I was there along with my new partner and co-owner Dennis, Dennis's dad Russ, my son Ollie, and my dad's brother Bobby, as well as Bobby's son Brian and a good friend of mine from Colfax, Barry

Rice. Both Brian and Barry had hunted with us previously. They had become a part of our permanent group and were in regular attendance. Robin was out of the state, working at a new job, and couldn't make it for the season. While Ollie traveled from school in Michigan to the shack, he hit a deer with his truck, providing us with camp meat at the beginning of the season.

Deer season that year came and went without much fanfare. We played the usual card games and ate great food, and although we managed to shoot a couple of deer during the hunt, there would be no tales of monster bucks being shot. Merle finally felt well enough to come up for one night, and it was great to have a Jolly Boy back in camp with us. Over the course of the season, there were more than just a few tears shed remembering my father. He had been a mentor to both of my sons, and they were having a very difficult time coming to grips with the fact that he would no longer be occupying his chair at the head of the table.

Toward the end of the season, Adder sent word that he wanted us to pack up all of his belongings at Blue Heaven and bring them back into town with us when we broke camp for the season. Although Adder would still make a trip or two to the shack over the years for an evening visit and dinner, he would never again occupy his bunk at Blue Heaven.

PRIME RIB OF BEEF ROAST

Whenever the Jolly Boys desired the ultimate festive evening meal at our hunting camp, they looked to prime rib to fill that need. Properly prepared and served with *au jus* and horseradish sauce, along with side dishes of garlic mashed potatoes and a great salad or asparagus wrapped in bacon, prime rib can make one feel as if they are dining at an exclusive supper club. It is nothing more than uncut rib eye steak that is still in the form of a roast, and rib eyes are said to be one of the most popular cuts of steak.

My father taught me three things about purchasing and preparing prime rib. The first thing I needed to learn was that when you go to the grocery store or meat market and ask to purchase a prime rib roast, you're probably not actually purchasing "prime" rib. Beef is graded according to the marbling in the meat, the small white swirls of fat within the meat, which make the beef tender and flavorful. "Prime" is the best grade and also the most expensive. More often than not, it needs to be special-ordered from a butcher in advance. Most butchers don't sell many prime cuts because of the price, so they rarely have a prime rib roast in their meat case. The majority of prime beef cuts are sold to only the most exclusive restaurants by the distributor. Most often, a butcher will have a "choice" prime rib roast on hand, and although it is a grade down from prime, it still has excellent marbling and is about half the cost of prime. After prime and choice are the "select" cuts of beef. Forget about select. It has very little marbling and is very lean. You can't purchase a bad cut of meat and make it better by cooking it. As the saying goes, you get what you pay for.

My father then taught me about purchasing the correct cut. The preferred cut is a standing rib roast. The bones have not been removed, and when you cook it, the ribs should be placed in the roasting pan bone-side down, with the fat side of the prime rib facing up so the fat juices of the meat penetrate the roast as it is cooking. Usually, the standing rib roast is only available around the major holiday seasons of Thanksgiving, Christmas, and New Year's Eve. During other times of the year, the roast is usually sold bone-out, but both are equally good. If you are fortunate and find a standing rib roast, figure that each rib will feed about two people. If you purchase a bone-out roast, figure about one-half to three-quarters of a pound of meat per person. There's considerable waste on a great prime rib roast.

Finally, I learned from my father how to prepare and cook the roast. He had a great deal of expertise in doing so.

Preparation

Use a sharp knife and score the top fat section of the roast in a diamond pattern, cutting into the fat about one-quarter inch deep. Use a liberal amount of fresh minced garlic or prepared garlic from the jar and rub the garlic down into the slits of the fat for flavoring. Also coat the top fat layer with a liberal amount of kosher salt and coarsely ground pepper. Place the roast in a shallow roasting pan, one that has edges about one to two inches high to catch the juices of the roast as it cooks. The juices will be used later to make *au jus* to serve with the roast.

Place the uncovered roast in a very hot preheated oven and cook it for about 15 minutes at 450 degrees. The extreme heat will sear the roast to lock in all the natural moisture. Reduce the oven temperature to 325 degrees, and allow about 15 minutes per pound to produce a medium-rare roast. Always use a meat thermometer to track the internal temperature of the roast. As a guide, when the center of the roast is

115–120 degrees, it is rare; at 130–135 degrees, it is medium-rare; and 140–145 degrees, it is medium. Keep in mind that when you remove the roast from the oven, it will still cook for a bit, so allow for a five- to ten-degree temperature rise once the roast is out of the oven and resting prior to being cut and served.

We find that most people prefer their prime rib either medium-rare or rare. When the internal temperature reaches 130 degrees (medium-rare), the center of the roast will be pink to red, while the end cuts will be brown. The rest of the roast will be medium-rare.

The three most important aspects in preparing the perfect prime rib roast are allowing the roast to rest before cutting and serving it, removing the roast from the oven before it becomes overcooked, and never piercing the roast with forks.

When your roast has reached the desired internal temperature, remove it from the roasting pan and place it on a serving platter with aluminum foil tented over the roast. Allow the roast to rest for about thirty minutes. If you cut and serve the roast immediately after removing it from the oven, the hot juices within the roast will bleed out and you will lose much of its flavor and tenderness. Always allow the roast to rest.

For the same reason, never use sharp serving forks to stab and place the roast in the baking pan or to remove the roast from the oven. You want to lock in all the natural juices. Any penetration of the roast during the cooking process will allow the natural juices to flow from the roast through those holes while it is cooking.

Finally, if your roast becomes overcooked, you can't fix it. It's better to remove the roast from the oven earlier rather than later because if the roast is slightly undercooked, it can be fixed with an easy trick. If some of your guests find that their serving is too rare for them, simply take their slice of prime rib using tongs and place it in simmering *au jus* for ten to fifteen seconds. A rare piece of prime rib will magically become medium-rare in a few seconds, and a medium-rare piece can be transformed into medium in the same time frame. It's always better to undercook than overcook a roast.

AU JUS AND HORSERADISH SAUCE

Preparation

While the roast is resting on a separate platter, place the roasting pan with the roast juices on the stovetop and use moderate heat to bring it to a simmer, scraping the bottom of the pan to blend everything together. Add about 3 cups of water and 1 tablespoon of beef bouillon paste along with 2 tablespoons of prepared horseradish. Once simmering, add either 1 cup of red wine or 1 cup of brandy to the mixture to kick things up a notch. Serve the *au jus* in small individual bowls and use the remaining *au jus* to quickly dip any prime rib that requires additional cooking.

Horseradish sauce is an elegant accessory to go with the prime rib and is prepared by combining 2 cups of sour cream and 1/4 to 1/2 cup of horseradish in a small bowl. Place in a serving dish and put it on the table.

Young Blood, 1995

In the early summer of 1995, the Sawyer County Conservation and Forestry Committee made a recommendation that the Recreational Use Permits for the one hundred cabins on county forestlands be included in the next ten-year forest management plan. We were all relieved that the lease for Blue Heaven would be safe for at least the next ten years. It seemed like the only group opposed to the permits was the Wisconsin DNR. I, like my father before me, penned a letter to the local newspaper praising the Forestry Committee for its decision to continue the permits and voicing my disapproval over the DNR's lack of cooperation and foresight to continue the camps.

The transition of the group coming to Blue Heaven continued in 1995 with the addition of Ollie's close friend, Brian Lane. We now had both Brian Hanson, who had been hunting with us for several years, and Brian Lane coming to the shack. In order to keep the confusion to a minimum, we nicknamed Brian Hanson "Billie-Bob" because he was an avid NASCAR fan, and we gave Brian Lane the nickname "City-Billy" because he hailed from the Twin Cities area. Although we all missed the Jolly Boys of yesteryear, Dennis and I were both thrilled to see the influx of younger hunters joining our group. We strongly felt that having younger men hunting with us would greatly increase our chances of getting more deer during deer season, and their assistance with all the camp chores would be most welcome.

Billie-Bob was the son of my father's brother Bobby. He had lost some favor with my father after an incident at the shack back in the mid-seventies. On his first visit to Blue Heaven, when he was in his early twenties, Billie-Bob had a wee bit too much to drink one evening and fell asleep at the table after everyone else had retired for the evening. Normally, someone falling asleep at the table wouldn't have been a problem, but he had loaded the woodstove with wood with the stove drafts wide open. My father awoke from deep slumber smelling the shack filling with smoke and hearing the fire roaring. He leaped from his bunk and rushed to the stove to turn the drafts off and secure the stove lid. This oversight was a cardinal sin in my father's eyes, and he calmly informed my Uncle Bobby that Brian would no longer be welcome at Blue Heaven. It took quite a number of years before my father finally felt that Brian was mature enough to come up to Blue Heaven again. It was a lesson learned and remembered. Once allowed back at camp, Brian quickly earned his way back into my father's good graces and became a valued member of the hunting shack.

All bunks were filled for the opening deer-hunting weekend that year, but once again, no Jolly Boys attended. We saw more deer sign in our area than we had seen in more than a decade. After three days of hunting, we had five deer hanging from the deer pole and the season proved to be a banner year for Wisconsin deer hunters. There were 684,944 licensed hunters in the woods that season and they bagged a total of 398,002 deer. That equates to a success ratio of about 58 percent, and we had nine hunters in our camp bagging five deer for a success ratio of 56 percent. Needless to say, we were pleased with our results and the management of the deer herd.

Merle and Adder came up for an evening of card playing and a great dinner of venison on the first Monday night of that season, but neither of them showed any interest in staying overnight at Blue Heaven. As they had walked into the bunk area to examine their old bunks, one could see that they were remembering days past at Blue Heaven. It felt like we were treating them as guests in their own home, and all of us felt strange as we watched them walk out the door and leave for town that evening. We had eleven around our table for dinner that night. For a moment, it seemed like the old dinner parties that the Jolly Boys used to have up at camp, but we never even came close to duplicating their antics at Blue Heaven.

Ghosts and Spooks

In late October of 1996, Ollie and his friend City-Billy, along with their friend Derrick decided to go up to the shack before the rest of us arrived so they could open up the camp and get the fires going. It was a cold and windy October evening and the three of them had arrived too late to think about preparing a dinner for themselves. They settled for drinks and snacks while they enjoyed a game of cards.

When the rest of us arrived for the annual fall work party the next morning, they related a story of an encounter that they all swore happened around midnight. The three of them had imbibed ample drinks and grown tired of playing cards, and they were talking about turning in for the night. Suddenly, a huge gust of wind buffeted the shack. The three of them simultaneously looked over at the window above the kitchen sink, where they saw what appeared to be a face peering through the window at them. Thinking that it might be one of us arriving late that evening, they all went outside to greet the new arrival but found no one there. They walked around the outside of the shack, but saw neither man nor beast lurking in the shadows. Naturally, they were somewhat shaken by this strange encounter. Ollie even speculated that it might have been the spirit of his grandfather peeking in at them as they enjoyed their evening at Blue Heaven. The shack log records their encounter in a poem.

'Twas the week before Halloween, and all around the shack
Ghosts and goblins haunted the door in the back.
Ollie, Brian, and Derrick had arrived the night before,
And swore there were ghosts peeking through the door.
Could it be real spooks, or brains that were numb
From late hours of drinking too much whiskey and rum?

After Merle, Dennis, Russ, Bobby, Billie-Bob, Barry, and I got settled in with our gear for the weekend, we all got busy completing various tasks around camp in preparation for the 1996 deer season. Once again we needed to relevel the shack; cut, split, and stack the wood; change the oil in the light plant; and perform numerous minor repairs.

We were just about ready to take a break and have our Saturday noon lunch, when appearing out of nowhere was an unclean-looking individual riding his bike up the logging trail to our shack. We were confused as to why someone would be riding a bike this deep in the woods. He wore a backpack and appeared to be homeless. He stopped, got off his bike, rolled and lit up a joint, and asked us if we wanted a hit. We all politely declined his offer and asked him what he was doing so deep in the woods. He responded that he was "looking for jack pines." The hunters of Blue Heaven knew that there weren't any jack pines within twenty miles. We pointed to the road and told him he would have to go back to the main highway and head north to find the trees he was looking for. He reeked of pot and we were all anxious for him to leave the area. He finally did leave. There was then considerable speculation as to whether he had been the spook appearing at the window the evening before. We were also concerned that he might have been eyeing up Blue Heaven as a place to live after we left for the weekend. Fortunately, we never saw him again.

CHURCH BARBECUES

I've always been amazed at how much food the younger guys
at our camp can go through when they sit down at the table.
Their hunger seems impossible to satisfy, and it's an unending
challenge to make certain that ample food is placed on the
table for their consumption. In years past, we usually served
fried hamburgers for lunch when we were at the shack in the
spring and fall for work parties. Some guys could easily polish
off three hamburgers. I therefore looked for a menu item that
would satisfy them, yet keep costs within our limited budget.
The answer came in my mother's "church barbecue" recipe. I
don't know who should receive the credit for this recipe. All
I can recall is my mother telling me that the recipe was developed by the ladies of her church to help stretch the hamburger
when they were making barbecues for a church function. It is
simple to prepare and the flavor is excellent. This recipe will,
I hope, serve 8 to 10 people.

Ingredients
4 pounds 80/20 ground beef
1 large yellow onion, diced
Salt and pepper
2 (10.5-ounce) cans condensed chicken gumbo soup
1 cup ketchup
1/4 cup yellow mustard

Preparation
Brown ground beef in a large skillet with onion. Liberally
salt and pepper while the meat is browning. Once the beef is
cooked and broken into small pieces, drain excess grease from
skillet. Add condensed soup, ketchup, and mustard. Do not

dilute soup with water. Stir and cover, allowing ingredients to simmer for about an hour.

Serve on hamburger buns, on paper plates with a fork. I usually just put the pot on the table and allow people to serve themselves, as some like to eat the barbecues "open-faced." A handful of potato chips and a good kosher dill pickle go well with these sandwiches.

I also often make an easy dip to go with the potato chips. This can be accomplished by taking a small container of chilled sour cream and adding a teaspoon of garlic salt, along with few good shakes of dill weed. Stir so the ingredients incorporate and allow it to sit chilled for about half an hour before serving.

Our War on Mice

Throughout the years, our hunting camp has been damaged by windstorms, hailstorms, vandalism, theft, porcupines, and other perils. Some of the most frustrating damages, however, have been caused by Mr. Mouse. Being in the middle of the woods and having the shack unoccupied for the majority of the year gives the advantage to these destructive little creatures that seem to take up occupancy as soon as we lock the door.

We deal with "deer mice," or, in scientific terms, *Peromyscus*. They have big eyes and little ears that look like deer ears, and they are very agile compared to the common house mouse. They are extremely industrious. These mice have light brown fur and a white underbelly and, to be honest, I find them to be somewhat cute.

Mr. Mouse started to appear in our hunting shack shortly after it was built. I recall being up there one weekend when my mother pulled open the silverware drawer, only to find Mrs. Mouse and her litter occupying the drawer in a nest built out of paper towels. After the screaming stopped, my father grabbed the drawer and threw the contents out in the leaves. The silverware was triple-washed by my mother, and then washed again. After all, these little guys are noted for being carriers of multiple diseases. A year or two later, she was again surprised to find a mouse nest, this time in our linen drawer. More screaming, more throwing of contents into the woods. My mother was a farm girl, familiar with all sorts of critters, but she didn't think that mice were "cute."

When I was a young man up at Blue Heaven, I always slept in the center upper bunk directly below an old moldy mounted deer head. One evening, as I crawled into my sleeping bag, I thought I had a vision that the old deer head was actually moving. Closer examination revealed that Mrs. Mouse and her large family had built a nest in the forehead of that old mount, which was teeming with activity. No screaming, but my father once again pitched valuable contents of the hunting shack out into the woods. The sad part is that the eight-point mount was the old buck head where we stuck our dollars for the hunter who shot the first buck. We now use a simple icepick to attach the dollar bills to the wall.

For years we tolerated the mice. After all, we had invaded their territory, and we had to cohabitate with them or burn the shack down. I even recall one night when the little guys were racing around on the open rafters in the ceiling. We had great sport trying to nail one of them with an icepick, but they were much too fast and agile for us. Our quest to control them with various traps and poisons also proved unsuccessful.

One fall weekend just before deer season 1998, Dennis Clagett went out to crank up the light plant because it was getting dark, and mice came running out of the light plant as it began to start. The light plant was cooled by a fan and radiator attached to the engine, and mice had built a nest inside the fan. Dennis came into the shack to announce his personal war on our mice. In the weeks and months that followed, he spent considerable time caulking cracks, plugging holes with steel wool, nailing boards over openings, setting traps, and putting out poison. This was war and he was going to win.

Dennis successfully controlled the mice around the camp for quite a number of years. With the amount of d-CON that he put in the area, most of us figured there wasn't a mouse within three miles. But about ten years after Dennis had completed his mouse-proofing efforts, the mice were back with a vengeance. Part of the problem was that the hunting shack was aging. Having been built on piers with only clay soil to support the place, the shack was settling, and new cracks and entry points provided opportunities for nesting and breeding. We had won the battle but not the war. More steel wool, more caulking, more d-CON, and more traps were put out.

During deer season 2005, my son Ollie decided it was time to intervene and came up with a solution for our mouse problems. He went on the Internet and found a new mouse trap aptly called "the Wheel of Death." It has been our salvation. The wheel is a simple contraption for eliminating mice. First, take an old bucket, poke a hole on opposite sides, and run a wire coat hanger through the holes. Then, punch holes through an empty tuna can with the lid still attached or an empty plastic pop bottle with the cap still on. The can or bottle is threaded and centered on the coat hanger in the middle of the bucket. This is the wheel, and the rigid coat hanger wire serves as the axle. Coat the wheel with peanut butter. Partially fill the bucket with six or more inches of old motor oil or antifreeze so the liquid doesn't freeze when the weather turns cold. Finally, lean a wooden stick up against the bucket to serve as a ramp for the mouse to climb up to the rim of the bucket. The mouse smells and sees the peanut butter and crawls out on the wire to the wheel. As soon as the mouse reaches the wheel, the wheel starts spinning and the mouse falls off the wheel into the motor oil or antifreeze, quickly drowning.

To add a little sport to the Wheel of Death, we started a pool to see who could guess how many mice would meet their demise over the course of the deer season. Everyone put in a dollar along with their guess. At the end of the season, we drained the pail and lying on the bottom were thirty-seven mice. Unbelievable! Barry won the pool with his guess of thirty-six.

The Wheel is probably not something that you would want sitting in the middle of your living room, but it works perfectly well for hunting shacks, garages, basements, and other areas where mice are abundant and need to be controlled.

Camp Elders, 1996–2000

As we entered the second half of the 1990s, Blue Heaven continued to see major changes concerning the hunters who were occupying its bunks. None of the original Jolly Boys attended any longer. Marvin, Kenny, and Howard had all passed away, and Merle and Adder had lost much of their desire to join us during deer season. The patriarchs of our camp now consisted of my dad's brother Bobby and Dennis's father, Russ Clagett. Everyone else was much younger. The faces around the poker table were all familiar, but everyone felt the absence of the original Jolly Boys.

On a Tuesday evening during deer season 1997, Adder was able to return to the shack with Merle for one last meal of Shack Steak. He was eighty-seven years old. It was fantastic to see both Adder and Merle, the last of the Jolly Boys, sitting at their usual spots at the poker table that evening. Shortly before deer season, Merle's son, JK, had passed away of a stroke at the very young age of forty-seven. John Kimball Dunster had been not only Merle's son but also my cousin and Dennis's brother-in-law. We all felt a huge void now that he was no longer with us. He had been a big part of Blue Heaven in the earlier years before he left to join several friends who had established Camp Handicapped. These hunters were all close friends of JK, and one of the members, Tom, had lost his leg in the Vietnam War. Another member, Rolf, had lost his arm in a childhood accident. JK was a very kind person, with a remarkable sense of humor, and we had always enjoyed his companionship. We missed having him at Blue Heaven after he made the decision to begin hunting with his friends.

JK frequently related a story about an evening when he and the other members of Camp Handicapped paid a visit to a gentleman's club named Phipps Tavern during deer season. One of the scantily dressed young ladies was dancing directly in front of their group, and they were trying to coerce her into coming back to their hunting camp for a "private showing." After much debate, the young lady finally lost her patience and told them, "Look, guys, it would take an arm and a leg for me to come back to your hunting shack with you." With that, Rolf took off his shirt, removed his artificial arm, and laid it on the bar. Then Tom slid off his artificial leg from underneath his jeans and laid it on the bar. Most of the other hunters in the bar had been witnessing these negotiations, and the place broke out in riotous laughter when Tom and Rolf attempted to pay her price with an arm and a leg.

JK's memory would live on with all of us at Blue Heaven because shortly after JK passed away, Merle gave my younger son, Ollie, JK's old Jeep, which had been sitting in JK's garage deteriorating for several years. He had purchased the used 1966 Willys CJ5 Jeep and had driven it for a number of years. When it began to fall into disrepair, he decided to park it in his garage, simply closing the garage door and leaving it there to rot. After Merle gave the Jeep to Ollie in the summer of 1998, Ollie put it on a car trailer and hauled it home to begin the tedious project of rebuilding the vehicle. The tires were old and flat, the wheels and brakes were no good, there was rust throughout, and the engine needed to be overhauled. Ollie and his friend Brian Lane spent the summer rebuilding JK's old Jeep and drove it in to the hunting shack during deer season of that year. We were all amazed at the transformation. Ollie and Brian had spent countless hours rebuilding that old Jeep, and they turned it into a completely functional showpiece. We added it to our arsenal of transportation used to maneuver around the mud holes on our way into the hunting camp.

In March 1998, Adder passed away in the comfort of his home sitting fully dressed at his kitchen table, with his morning prune juice in front of him. He was such a big part of our hunting camp for more than forty years and was always overjoyed to be at Blue Heaven, even if it was only for an evening to take part in a game of poker while sipping on a Manhattan. He constantly reminisced about his many great memories of Blue Heaven, as well as the hunting camps of old. He left us with many stories about the history of Hayward. He seemed to know everyone and how they fit into the history of the area. We all regretted that he had not taken the time to put those stories on paper or cassette, even though we had encouraged him to do so. A true historian, he possessed knowledge that was unequaled. Our hunting camp sent a huge bouquet of blue flowers to his well-attended funeral, along with a poem that summed up our love of this man.

> Thanks for the memories, for all those stories you shared;
> Thanks for having been with us, we'll miss how much you
> cared.
> Thanks for giving us those traditions we cherish at hunting
> camp;
> We'll miss your wisdom and your company when we light
> the Aladdin lamp.
> Thanks for everything that you left us to remember;
> You will always be among us when we gather in November.

Shortly after Adder's passing, we learned that Russ Clagett had developed a serious medical condition called Wegener's granulomatosis and he sadly succumbed to the disease, which attacks a person's vital organs. Once again, we all found ourselves coping

John, Dennis, Ollie, Mike Schaaf, Brian Hanson, Barry Rice, and Robin enjoy drinks and poker during one of the final deer seasons at Old Blue.

with the loss of one of the icons of our hunting camp. Russ had become a true honorary Jolly Boy after hunting with us for almost thirty years and had enthusiastically participated in the hunting camp right up to his end. He was an excellent hunter, and his game of choice at the poker table was deuces wild. He had cherished our camp traditions and the fellowship and honor of being a part of our group at Blue Heaven, and we were blessed to have had him as a part of the hunting camp.

Our group changed considerably during this period. Ollie's brother-in-law at that time, Nate, began hunting with us during deer season 1997, and Ollie's friend Brian "City-Billy" Lane also became regularly involved. Although we were rapidly losing many of the camp elders, younger and more energetic hunters were now filling the vacated bunks and learning about the traditions and rules that applied to our beloved hunting camp. Dennis and I were beginning to realize that we were now the camp elders, even though we didn't necessarily want that honor.

As the end of the decade approached, the shack log shows that our group began to see the fruits of all the younger hunters hunting out of the camp each fall. In 1999, we harvested four deer. Even though we had seven either-sex permits, we decided not to shoot any more deer that year because the weather was very warm, with daytime temperatures reaching into the midsixties. We already had deer waiting to be cut up and put into coolers on ice due to the warm weather, and we didn't want to have any of our coveted venison spoil. In 1999, we harvested six bucks. The deer herd appeared to be in great abundance. We had multiple either-sex permits that had not yet been filled, but we had taken the deer we needed, and all agreed not to shoot any more deer unless it was a trophy buck. Deer season 2000 was a near repeat of 1999, and we had seven deer hanging on the deer rack outside. Once again, we decided that we had all the venison we needed and that we would allow the remaining deer herd in our area to be left undisturbed. We hoped this would allow the herd to perpetuate itself and assure successful deer seasons in the coming years. The Jolly Boys had taught us well: harvest only what you need for your own use. Respect nature and what it has to offer. Never get greedy so that you will have deer in your area for the coming years and generations.

DEER SEASON 1996 CAMP LOG ENTRIES

Volume II of our shack log provides very specific details of the 1996 deer season at Blue Heaven. The entries are representative of most deer seasons. I quote directly from the log to provide the flavor of what actually happens during a typical nine-day deer hunt:

> Friday 11/22/96—John, Dennis, Russ, Barry & Bobby
> arrive about 3 p.m. via Coot to open camp. Road is frozen

and in good shape. About 3″ of snow on ground. Everyone gets busy putting away supplies and John asks Russ, "Where are the 50 pounds of the 'Best Yet' potatoes you bought in Exeland?" Russ checks all his pockets, turns pale, and begins staring at floor. Dennis puts on coat and makes two hour trip to Russ' house on Chief Lake to pick up 50# of potatoes. Billie-Bob arrives at 4:30 via his new-but-used '93 Ford Ranger 4X4 with optional pizza cutter tires and heated rear bumper. Dennis Skare is also in attendance checking out the movement into deer camp. Skare leaves to buy deer license and blaze orange equipment and promises to return on Sunday to hunt. Violet's meatballs, boiled rutabagas and Russ' "well-traveled" potatoes for supper. All settle down about 11 p.m. to rest for opening day only to be awakened by Ollie and Robin arriving at 2 a.m. via noisy Dodge 4X4. Robin arrived from twin cities on Sun Country charter at 10:30 p.m. to ride up with Ollie. Ollie brings along two Minnesota deer killed on recent trip to Boundary Waters in northern Minnesota during the Minnesota deer season. Two deer are hanging from the deer pole and no one has even loaded a rifle yet!

Saturday 11/23/96—Eight sleepy hunters stumble into woods attempting to fill meat rack. We have four either-sex permits. **** hits fan while Ollie is at the Birch and Ollie slays one of four deer and wounds another. Large doe is added to meat rack and attempt is made to track down wounded deer after pancake, egg and sausage breakfast. Appears wounded deer has minor leg wound and although John and Ollie get close, deer escapes all attempts to issue a final blow. Merle makes several calls on camp phone from highway requesting updates on the hunt. All enjoy ribs, kraut and best traveled potatoes for dinner.

Sunday 11/24/96—Another attempt is made to track down Ollie's wounded deer with no success. John meets up with

Darrell Slama and daughter Rachel from Club 27 while hunting
and both stop in to see Blue Heaven and enjoy a refreshment.
~~Merle calls and Rachel answers camp phone explaining she is~~
new dancing girl. Merle hangs up phone very confused thinking he dialed wrong number. Dennis Skare arrives sporting new
blaze orange hunting outfit, his first Wisconsin deer license and
carrying borrowed rifle from Merle. Skare is posted by horse
barn where he proceeds to contaminate the woods and his new
hunting outfit after over-indulging on eggs at breakfast. Skare
leaves deer camp after his two hour hunt grumbling that no one
should be allowed to have this much fun. DNR special contam-
ination team is brought in to decontaminate Birch Street. Rob
and Ollie are fed Violet's left-over meatballs with Shack Peas for
supper as they have to return to twin cities. Rest of us dine on
spaghetti and garlic French bread later. Dennis and Barry have
marathon dish washing event. Billie-Bob wins all the money at
the poker game.

Monday 11/25/96—Weather is turning colder. Highs in
the teens and lows are sub-zero. Lots of fresh sign below the
Birch and by the Horse Barn but no more deer. Billie-Bob
picks up Adder and Merle at 5 p.m. for their visit to camp.
Served Shack Steak made with Ollie's Minnesota deer along
with potatoes and Shack Peas for dinner following a fun game
of poker where Barry and John win all the money. Monday
morning had been spent cutting up one of Ollie's deer and
starting the pot of vegetable beef soup. Had Violet's left-over
meatballs over bread for brunch.

Tuesday 11/26/96—Clear and cold. Mid-teens for the
daytime high. Quite a bit of deer sign but still no new deer.
Bobby spends much of afternoon "sipping" and quickly
becomes Mr. El-Blasto by early evening. Lester Schaaf arrives late p.m. to partake in festivities and loses deer rifle
and pickup in poker game. (Only kidding.) Appears Lester

spent much of p.m. having a few to take the edge off as he's
Mr. Smiley on arrival in camp. Left-over spaghetti for supper
with Italian salad and garlic toast. Dennis and Billie-Bob play
guest chefs in shack kitchen and made several ****-ups in
the attempt. Lester is given sponge bath by Dennis to clean
off spaghetti on hands and face and then steered into center
middle bunk via Adder's Ladder. Very obvious to all that the
drunk fairy made a visit to Blue Heaven and tapped her magic
wand on Bobby and Lester. Bobby wins all the money and
once again declares "first time ever" win of show-down game.
Rest of evening spent attempting to clean table cloth around
Lester's plate.

Wednesday 11/27/96—Everyone departs for Thanksgiving except for Dennis, Russ and Barry. Dinner of left-over
Shack Steak, meatballs, potatoes and Shack Peas. Barry wins
all the money in poker game.

Thursday 11/28/96—Barry leaves camp leaving Dennis
and Russ alone for Thanksgiving dinner which Barbara had
brought out to them. Both spend day doing a little hunting
and taking care of many chores around camp including the
skinning and cutting up of one of Ollie's Minnesota deer.
Ollie and his friend Brian Lane return to camp about 2 a.m.

Friday 11/29/96—Merle makes inspection trip to camp
and returns to town after a cup of coffee. Bobby, Billie-Bob
and John arrive later in a.m. Left-over vegetable soup for
brunch. Derrik pays visit to camp and stays for snacks and
poker game. Russell wins all the money and declares Derrik
his favorite gaming person after Derrik contributes heavily to
Russ' winnings. We dine on probably the best venison loins
ever along with Shack Green Beans and potatoes. Weather
has warmed and brought rain which turns to snow that is
sticking to everything. Brian "camp houseboy" Lane wins
show-down game.

Saturday 11/20/96—Everyone, except our houseboy, goes out for the hunt in woods wet with snow that has stuck to everything. Several hot tracks are followed with no luck. Russ gets a shot at a deer and Bobby sees a deer and immediately returns to camp to start celebrating. Four pounds of bacon, blueberry pancakes and eggs for brunch. Afternoon is spent cutting up Ollie's big doe shot at the Birch. Poker game lasting until 10 p.m. followed by venison loins served with green pepper, mushrooms and onions and Shack Baked Potatoes. Ollie becomes exhausted and sneaks into his bunk at 9:15 and misses supper. John wins the final show-down game.

VEGETABLE BEEF SOUP WITH DUMPLINGS

There's probably nothing more satisfying for a noon lunch during deer camp when it's cold and windy outside than a hearty bowl of soup or stew. After the first few days of deer camp, most of us get tired of the traditionally huge lumberjack-style breakfast involving eggs with breakfast meat and want to have a more traditional meal when we arrive back at camp for our noon break. Vegetable beef soup with dumplings is always a big hit. We make a huge pot of it, so there is an ample amount for leftovers with saltines and plenty of butter. This recipe will serve 6–8 hungry hunters for at least two meals. Purchase an inexpensive cut of beef roast. And don't bother with soup bones—there's no meat on soup bones!

Ingredients

3- or 4-pound pot roast
2 tablespoons chicken bouillon paste (do not use broth or cubes)
1/2 tablespoon salt
1/2 tablespoon ground black pepper
1 large yellow onion
1/2 stalk celery
1 (2-pound) package carrots
1 large rutabaga
3 large potatoes

Preparation

Fill a 12-quart stock pot half full with water and bring to a simmer. Put the pot roast into the water and add chicken bouillon paste, salt, and pepper. (Don't oversalt the broth; the chicken bouillon has an intense salt flavor also.) Slice the celery into quarter-inch pieces, and dice the yellow onion; add both to the pot. Simmer for 3 or 4 hours until the pot roast becomes falling-apart tender. Sample the broth after it has simmered for a couple of hours to determine whether more salt or chicken bouillon is needed. If so, add additional salt or bouillon to taste. If overly salty, add more water to the pot to dilute.

Once the pot roast is cooked, pull it from the broth and put it on a plate. Remove any fat from the roast and then use a fork to shred the roast by pulling the fork through the meat. Discard fat, put the shredded pot roast back into the pot, and continue to simmer.

Peel and chop the rutabaga into half-inch cubes and add to the pot. Rutabaga takes a long time to cook, so this should be added to the broth for simmering about 45 minutes before adding the carrots and potatoes.

Peel and cut the carrots into half-inch slices and add to the pot. Peel and dice the potatoes into half-inch cubes and add them to the pot. Allow this mixture to simmer for about an hour until all the vegetables become very tender.

Once the soup is fully cooked and the broth has passed your taste test, it's time to make the dumplings (see below). Make certain that there is ample broth in the pot, as dumplings will soak up a lot of the broth as they are cooking. Dumplings are very easy to make, and they will add a dimension of heartiness to the soup.

DUMPLINGS

Ingredients

3 cups all-purpose flour
1 teaspoon salt
4 eggs
2 cups boiling water

Preparation

Place flour in a mixing bowl. Stir in salt. Beat four eggs in a separate cup. Add the eggs to the flour and salt and mix thoroughly. Quickly add boiling water to the mixture and stir rapidly to prevent the eggs from turning into scrambled eggs. The mixture will be the consistency of a heavy paste. Bring the soup to a moderate rolling boil and use a spoon to drop the dumpling mixture into the boiling soup broth, alternating the positioning of the dumplings so they don't stick together. Once the dumplings have been deposited in the broth, cover the pot with a lid and allow them to cook in the moderately boiling broth for about 15 minutes. As the dumplings cook, they will float to the surface of the soup, and the dumpling mixture will actually double or triple in size.

Put the entire pot on the table, using pot holders or a cutting board to protect the tabletop from the heat of the pot. Use a ladle to serve the soup in large soup bowls, and serve to your hungry hunters with lots of saltines and butter.

The dumplings will all be consumed during the first serving of this lunch favorite, so be prepared to mix up another batch of dumplings when the leftover soup is served on another day!

VENISON STEW

Another noontime hit with all of our hungry hunters is venison stew. This can be made with either fresh venison or venison steak that is already cooked and has been left over from a previous dinner. It's also an excellent way to use any venison left over from a previous deer season that's been sitting in your freezer and is starting to get old. This recipe will feed 6–8 people and is wonderful served with warmed buns and lots of butter.

Ingredients

3 to 4 pounds venison round steak cut from the hindquarter of the deer and cubed into bite-sized portions, about 3/4 to 1 inch
1/4 cup (1/2 stick) Parkay or a similar product
1 large yellow onion
1 tablespoon beef bouillon paste (do not use broth or cubes)
1 (2-pound) package carrots
4 large potatoes
3 bay leaves
1 tablespoon prepared horseradish
Salt and pepper
Flour, corn starch, or Wondra Flour

Preparation

After cutting the venison into cubes and trimming off any tallow or fat, place the cubes in large frypan with Parkay. Brown all sides of the venison on medium heat, stirring frequently. (If leftover venison is being used, simply heat the venison in the Parkay without allowing it to overcook.) Chop the onion into large pieces and add to the venison while it is still frying.

Liberally salt and pepper the venison and onion. Once the venison and onion mixture has been browned, transfer it to a pot; cover the mixture with water and bring it to a simmer. Add a tablespoon of beef paste and blend it in. Put in the bay leaves and horseradish. Cover the pot and allow to simmer for 1 to 2 hours.

While the venison stew is simmering, peel the carrots and potatoes and chop them into 3/4- to 1-inch cubes. Place the carrots and potatoes into a separate pot with salted water and boil them until they are tender. Once tender, drain and add the carrots and potatoes to the stew. Add more water, if needed, to cover all ingredients. Simmer for an additional half hour. Thicken the liquid in the stew by placing equal parts of water and flour or water and corn starch in a small container with a lid, and shaking the mixture to remove lumps. Bring the stew up to a rapid simmer and slowly add the thickening agent to the stew broth until the preferred consistency is reached. (You can also use a product called Wondra Flour, which is a presifted flour used for thickening sauces. If Wondra is used, simply shake the flour into the beef broth while it is simmering rapidly, stirring constantly until the preferred consistency has been obtained.)

Remove the bay leaves and serve the stew in large soup bowls along with fresh bakery buns and lots of butter. Have the salt and pepper shakers handy for anyone who prefers additional seasoning.

An Uncertain Future,
2001–2003

Although the deer season in the fall of 2000 proved to be unusually warm and uneventful, Mother Nature did a turnabout shortly afterward. Because of numerous snowstorms, we were all concerned about the snow load on the aging shack roof, as there had been many reports of roofs collapsing under the weight of the snow in the area. Several members of our hunting camp went into the shack by snowmobile to shovel off the roof, which had almost three feet of snow on it. They also installed a brace inside the shack to help support the roof in the event that this weather pattern continued. The building was now forty-five years old, and time and previous harsh winters had made the roof a swayback. It was always a cause for concern.

Deer season 2001 also brought with it unusually warm weather. We shot two bucks on opening morning of deer season, placing a tarp tent over the buck pole to keep the deer out of the sun. By the first Tuesday of that season, we once again had seven deer hanging from the buck pole and once again declared that any additional deer should only be shot in a trophy buck situation. That season, there was considerable conversation during our evening poker games about chronic wasting disease (CWD), which had been discovered in the deer population in the southern part of the state. Although none of the deer in our area had been diagnosed with CWD, we were very concerned because the jury was still out on whether it was safe to consume the venison. As a result, we made the decision to discontinue our practice of eating pickled venison heart and fried venison liver. As a precaution, we also started to wear rubber gloves when dressing out the deer taken during the hunt.

The following deer season, 2002, Dennis and I saw only the younger hunters showing up for the hunt. My uncle Bobby had elected not to attend deer camp, as he was coping with a bad knee and felt it in his best interest to stay home. The conversations at the table during this season primarily concentrated on the future of Blue Heaven for our generation and generations to come. There had been many talks between Sawyer County Board members and the Sawyer County Forestry Department about the possibility of discontinuing the Recreational Use Permits in our county. Deep down, we knew that that decision was inevitable. Surrounding counties had already made the decision to discontinue the permits and it was only a matter of time before Sawyer County would do the same. Much discussion followed concerning options for our group, including purchasing a small portion of land nearby to which we could move Blue Heaven.

We decided that we would all explore what might be available in the area, and discussed how to dismantle and move the building once a new location had been found. In March of 2003, I wrote a letter to the Sawyer County Board and the Sawyer County Forestry Department outlining the importance of the hunting camps to the one hundred remaining permit holders and encouraging them to continue with the practice of the Recreational Use Permits. The following month, my mother, Violet, the last surviving Jolly Girl, passed away at the age of eighty-five. The end of the era of the "Greatest Generation" was coming more rapidly than any of us wanted to admit.

Deer season 2003 started out very slowly but ended up being successful. Opening weekend was warm, with no snow on the ground. However, on Monday it turned colder and we received eight inches of snow. The new snow generated a great deal of excitement, and that afternoon Brian Lane shot two large eight-point bucks and a large doe at the Ravine. We were able to harvest three more deer that season, thanks to the snow on the ground.

We also tried a new recipe up at camp that year. Ollie had been in South Dakota that fall and brought to camp eight pheasants that he had shot. Normally, our menu at deer camp avoided poultry. Thanksgiving always fell during deer hunting week, and everyone filled up on turkey. That year, however, we made an exception and experienced some very fine dining with "pheasant under cast-iron," garlic mashed potatoes, and Violet's superb cabbage-apple salad.

PHEASANT UNDER CAST-IRON

This recipe works equally well for pheasants, partridge, or quail. All have a delicate dry meat that requires slow cooking at low heat in the gravy to keep the meat moist. This recipe serves 8.

Ingredients
8 birds, washed and with birdshot removed
1/4 cup (1/2 stick) butter
2 (10.5-ounce) cans condensed cream of mushroom
    soup (or 3 cans Dawn Fresh Mushroom Sauce)
2 cups half & half
1 (8-ounce) can mushroom stems and pieces
Salt and pepper

Preparation

Cut the birds lengthways in half and place them in a nonstick frypan after slowly melting the butter. Salt and pepper the birds to taste. Slowly fry the birds on both sides until lightly browned. While the birds are frying, use a saucepan and mix the mushroom soup or mushroom sauce, along with the half & half and the can of mushrooms. Slowly heat the mixture but do not bring to a simmer. When the birds are brown and the gravy is warmed, place the birds in a cast-iron Dutch oven. If a Dutch oven is not available, use a regular roasting pan. We use the Dutch oven in the wood cookstove at deer camp, but a regular roasting pan is also suitable. Pour the gravy mixture over the birds, and cover the pan tightly while the birds are cooking to keep them as moist as possible. If your lid doesn't fit tightly, use aluminum foil to seal. Cook in the oven at 275 to 300 degrees for about 2 hours.

GARLIC MASHED POTATOES

Garlic mashed potatoes are as easy to make as regular mashed potatoes. Naturally, the secret ingredient is garlic. Use an ample amount. We take two whole bulbs of garlic cloves and cut off the root end. We then saturate the bulbs with olive oil and wrap them in aluminum foil. The garlic can then be roasted in the oven along with the birds. Just before serving dinner, using a mixer or a potato masher, mash up your boiled potatoes along with about a cup of milk, a quarter pound of butter, and the cooked garlic. Add the garlic bulbs by removing them from the foil and squeezing the cooked garlic cloves out of their skins into the potatoes. Mix well.

VIOLET'S CABBAGE-APPLE SALAD

Ingredients

1 small head of cabbage
1 cup Miracle Whip salad dressing
1 tablespoon sugar
2 Red Delicious apples

Preparation

Chop the cabbage into coleslaw-sized pieces and place in a large mixing bowl. Core the apples, chop into small pieces, and add to the cabbage. (Always use Red Delicious apples. Other apples are too tart!) Add the salad dressing to the cabbage, sprinkling it with the sugar. Blend all ingredients and chill. More salad dressing and sugar can be added if needed.

Serve the birds and gravy over the garlic mashed potatoes and use the salad as a side dish. One could easily substitute wild rice for the mashed potatoes, but you would then miss out on all that wonderful gravy to go with the mashed potatoes!

Financing a Hunting Camp

One of the key elements to the success of a hunting camp is pay-
ing the bills connected with its operation while at the same time
making the experience affordable. The Jolly Boys developed a per
diem charge when they established Blue Heaven. Each hunter was
assessed five dollars per day to cover the costs of groceries, beer,
supplies, taxes, insurance, and permit fees. Naturally, these costs
continued to escalate over the years. By the late 1990s, we charged
twenty-five dollars per day and even that fee did not fully cover
the expenses. The Recreational Use Permit was then costing us
five hundred dollars per year, with an additional five hundred dollars per year placed in escrow to help defray the costs of removing
the camps of those who chose to simply walk away when their
permits were discontinued.

Accordingly, at a meeting during deer season 2002, we all
agreed that our daily fee would increase to thirty dollars to cover
the costs of food and other supplies. Each regular member of our
group would pay an additional one hundred fifty dollars per year
to cover the fixed costs of taxes, insurance, and the permit. We
agreed that this was fair for all and necessary to keep our financial
situation solvent. Everyone who hunted at Blue Heaven knew that
there was no profit being realized from what was charged. We all
felt that thirty dollars was still a bargain, given all the great food

we were consuming and the accommodations that were being afforded. At the end of each deer season, the camp checkbook would be down to the bare bones, except for a few hundred dollars left in the account for emergencies. This became a problem as we began to discuss the possibility of purchasing land and moving the camp should the county eliminate the Recreational Use Permits.

Elimination of the Permits, 2004–2005

Deer season 2004 was a huge success. We harvested a ten-point buck, an eight-point, a six-point, and two spike bucks along with four large does. It was the most deer ever taken out of our hunting camp during deer season, and we rejoiced in our good fortune. Sadly, that deer season would be remembered for a senseless tragedy in the Rice Lake area. A hunter from Minnesota got into an argument with several hunters who had a camp near where he decided to hunt near Rice Lake, and the argument turned violent. The Minnesota hunter shot and killed five of the hunters from that camp and wounded three others. One of the wounded also died later that week. Every deer hunter in Wisconsin was outraged over this event, and a huge outpouring of donations was sent to a bank in Rice Lake to assist the families of the victims. To this day, no one can understand why this happened.

Shortly after deer season 2004, we received a letter from Mike Krueger, forest administrator for Sawyer County. He thought the cabins on county forestlands would be safe until 2011, but gave us no assurances that the county board would approve extending the permits beyond that date.

This was followed by a huge county board meeting on November 1, 2004, with more than 125 people in attendance voicing their opinions on the camp permit issues. Sawyer County was the only county in the state without a phase-out plan for the permits. Washburn County had only thirty-five remaining cabins, Polk County had only twelve permits, and Rusk and Clark Counties each had only six or seven permits. The Sawyer County Board expressed great concern that if they continued to issue the permits against the will of the DNR, they could lose substantial timber revenue from the county forestlands.

By January of 2005, the county board discussed possibly obtaining an outside legal opinion regarding the legality of the permits, but most board members opposed using taxpayer money to hire an attorney. The board knew they were under the gun to develop a new ten-year comprehensive forest-management plan, and it seemed likely that the camp permits would not be a part of that plan.

Worried about the discontinuation of our camp permit in the not-too-distant future and knowing we were in charge of our own destiny concerning Blue Heaven, I wrote a letter to Darrell Slama. He was one of the owners of Club 27, the hunting camp about a mile to the west of our current location. Darrell and several other men owned 36.37 acres of land, and their deer camp was just on the opposite side of the highway from ours, in the northwest portion of their property. The majority of their land was on our side of the highway, and we decided it would be ideal if they sold us enough land in the southwest corner of their acreage that we could relocate our hunting camp. My lengthy letter to Darrell outlined our dilemma in great detail. I enclosed copies of the numerous articles that had been written in local papers along with a copy of a plat map indicating the portion of their property we wished to purchase. I also enclosed several copies of my correspondence so Darrell could share my proposal with the other members of Club 27.

About a week after I sent my letter to Darrell in January of 2005, Sawyer County joined the other twenty-eight counties in Wisconsin that had agreed to discontinue private hunting camps on county land. There had been an enormous amount of confusion over the interpretation of the law under Wisconsin State Statute 28.11, and the county board felt that hiring an attorney to explore this law further was not feasible, given the fact that Sawyer County was the only county in the state still allowing the permits. The Sawyer County Board voted 12–3 to end the permits, and the sunset date for the removal of the hunting camps from Sawyer County forestlands was set at December 31, 2010. We were devastated by this decision. We realized that we had only five short years in which to locate and purchase property, move the camp, and reestablish it at the new location if we wanted to keep Blue Heaven from becoming just a memory.

From that point forth, every time we got together, the hunters of Blue Heaven talked about available options. Ollie had purchased a forty-acre plot of wild land several miles to our north, which was given heavy consideration. However, that location was too far away to allow us to hunt the hallowed grounds on which we had been hunting for the past fifty years. We needed to find something closer. No one wanted to hunt anywhere except where we were currently hunting. It was sacred to us; so much so that Dennis had even spread a portion of his father's ashes in an area where Russ used to spend late afternoons hunting, sitting on the side of a hill overlooking a swamp, and watching the sun set behind the hemlock pine trees. This area was familiar to us, and we had honored it for half a century, giving names to the logging roads and landmarks within the area. We even considered moving the shack onto a mobile home trailer and taking the shack back to that location for deer season every year. Unfortunately, the logistics of that plan seemed too complicated to make it practical. We also checked with all the local real estate agents, asking them to try to locate a nearby parcel of land for us. None was to be had, and the local property owners did not appear to have much interest in selling any of their property. Ultimately, we decided that our best option would be to continue to try to convince Club 27 to sell us a few acres in the southeast corner of their land. It was within a quarter mile of our present location and would be ideal.

Blue Heaven's
Fiftieth Anniversary

On Friday, November 18, 2005, the hunters of Blue Heaven gathered at deer camp to celebrate our fiftieth year at the hunting shack. It was quite a feat. The Jolly Boys' dream had perpetuated itself for five decades and the camp was still going strong. Many things had changed over the years, but it seemed that the more they changed, the more they stayed the same. We were all very proud that our camp was still intact after all these years, and felt that a party to celebrate the event certainly was in order.

We were greeted at the camp by four inches of new snow on the ground and a coating on all the trees. The woods looked beautiful. Although we didn't see many fresh deer tracks in the area, we saw an abundance of wolf tracks as well as signs that a bear or two were still wandering around, not yet settled in for their long winter's nap. That night, we dined on huge plates of Reali spaghetti and French bread garlic toast. A Caesar salad had been on the menu but was not made. Someone had eaten all the anchovies with the rest of the snacks that had been put out beforehand, and one couldn't possibly enjoy a Caesar salad without an ample amount of anchovies. The temperature was ideal, in the low thirties, and every hunter was settled in his bunk by 11 p.m. to get a good night's rest before the season opener the next morning.

We spent many hours in the woods on Saturday, but no one saw any deer. It was very disappointing to have been "skunked" on the season opener. But Sunday was a different story. Ollie shot two large does from his tree stand at the Birch early that morning, and Dennis bagged a spike buck soon afterward to give himself a birthday present. His birthday fell during deer season every year, and he had spent most of the day mumbling something about "a birthday buck." We purposely quit hunting early that day to return to the shack to prepare for our fiftieth anniversary party.

Merle, the last surviving Jolly Boy, and Bobby Hanson, arrived at 4 p.m. to join us in the celebration via the Coot driven by Dennis. Both were having ambulatory difficulties, along with other assorted health issues, but neither would have missed this party. Bobby was eager to get the poker game afoot, and Merle pulled out several old photo albums to share the memories of the good old days at Blue Heaven. Merle also brought in anniversary hats that he had made for everyone to wear, and Rob produced special T-shirts he had secretly ordered. A vast array of snacks was set out for everyone to enjoy during the card game. In the old cookstove, I prepared a huge, succulent, medium-rare bone-in prime rib roast heavily encrusted with an olive oil and crushed garlic topping, along with garlic mashed potatoes and a salad loaded with homemade bleu cheese dressing and bleu cheese crumbles. It was a meal fit for a king, and we wished that all the Jolly Boys of old could have been in attendance for this special occasion.

Very content, Merle and Bobby left camp that evening about 8 p.m. Neither one was in physical condition to spend any overnights at camp any longer. We drove them back to town to make certain that they arrived home safely. It was very sad to watch them drive out of sight on that old logging road after the party. We knew that, in all probability, that evening would be the last time either of them would be at the hunting camp they both loved so much.

Merle, the last surviving Jolly Boy, during his final trip to Blue Heaven on November 20, 2005, for the camp's fiftieth anniversary

Final Seasons at Blue Heaven, 2006–2008

We spent the final deer seasons at the old hunting shack in a slightly somber mood. The fact that we were losing the camp was always in the back of our minds. Plans had to be made to pack up everything, and more plans would have to be made as to where to store the contents of the shack until a new location could be found. It would be a major undertaking, and the uncertainty of our future was the only thing dampening our spirits during these last few seasons at the old shack.

On the first morning of deer season 2006, the light plant was fired up at 3:30 a.m., to everyone's shock and dismay. Someone from the bunk area yelled, "Don't ya think you're getting a little anxious?!" As it turned out, Ollie had set his alarm clock incorrectly, having been off by about an hour and a half. The light plant was turned off and, traumatized by the experience, we all finally drifted back to sleep until almost 6 a.m.

We saw lots of deer sign in the woods on Saturday, but no deer. On Sunday, Rob shot a spike buck at the Big Rock and, almost simultaneously, I shot a five-point buck by the Little Rocks. These shots could be heard by the other hunters. There was much debate about who had the right to the buck money for the first buck taken, but one of our hunters had been posted between the two of us and confirmed that Rob had indeed shot first. We had another successful season that year, harvesting a total of seven deer. Naturally, there were more discussions about the future of the hunting shack, but we reached no decisions.

We had a superb deer season in 2007, shooting a camp record of nine deer that year. Although we disliked the thought of having to give up our hallowed hunting grounds, Ollie's parcel of forty acres several miles north was beginning to look like our only option.

But fortune, it seemed, was on our side. During deer season 2008 my cousin, Brian Hanson, met one of the Club 27 hunters in the woods. The man's nickname was "Beach," and he told Brian that members of Club 27 had met and decided that they were willing to sell us a portion of their property, although they needed to find replacement property before doing so. Because their camp was incorporated, the sale would have tax consequences unless they located replacement property. Brian returned to camp that afternoon with the great news, knowing that this would be the perfect solution to our problem. The weather that deer season was excellent, and we ended up taking three bucks and three large does. The only thing that overshadowed the season was the fact that the last of our Jolly Boys, Merle Dunster, had been admitted to a nursing home, as his health was deteriorating and he was no longer capable of caring for himself.

End of an Era, 2009

There was no "fall frolic" in the fall of 2009. It was decided that there was no point in cutting firewood or making any repairs to the shack, because deer season 2009 would be the last season we would hunt out of Blue Heaven. We were still trying to conclude a deal with Club 27 to acquire enough of their land to relocate the shack, but things were still uncertain. We developed a backup plan to move the shack to Ollie's forty acres some six miles north of our current location. My older son, Rob, was aggressively leading negotiations with the members of Club 27, who still had some concerns over the sale.

When deer season 2009 arrived, the mood was decidedly different from previous deer seasons. My wife, Kathy, a staff reporter for the *Sawyer County Record* newspaper in Hayward, had listened to all the moaning, complaints, and expressions of disappointment about the loss of Blue Heaven. She wrote a column about our deer camp, and it was published shortly after the 2009 deer season. It drew many comments from readers, some of whom had never hunted deer. Her words evoked the traditions and nostalgia of our deer-hunting camp and brought tears to the eyes of many readers. The column, called "Goodbye 'Blue Heaven,' we will miss you," is framed and hangs above my desk in Hayward. It reads:

> Once again this November, I bore witness to my husband
> John readying for the deer hunt. It is a long, laborious and

protracted procedure, this getting ready for the hunt, and I have grown familiar with the preparations that go into it.

I have also, through the years, grown weary with the preparations that go into it.

It begins in our house about a month before opening day. The guys from the deer camp send their checks to John, who acts as the camp bookkeeper. For the next 30 days, John lines his den with boxes of gear and essentials. Old flannel pillowcases and mismatched sheets, hunting clothing I see only once a year, polished guns, shirts that hold dear memories for him that are lost on me—all are reverently brought out for the hunting season. The revered shack log—where entries dating back to the 1950s record the weather, the hunt, the kill and who lost most at poker—is carefully packed. Numerous lists of ingredients for the artfully-planned menus for every meal, starting with opening day and ending with the Sunday after Thanksgiving, are planned down to the last garlic clove. These meals are not hastily put together, nor are they cheap. There are 50-year old traditions that call for ribs and kraut on a certain evening; prime rib on another and Reali spaghetti made with pork ribs the next night. I could fill an entire column about the meals and you would ask for those recipes, but that isn't what I want to say here.

This year is different because it is the last time my husband and his friends will hunt on their beloved county land with the old shack still standing. The provision to allow cabin permit holders on county forest land has come to an end. On January 26, 2005, the Sawyer County Record reported that the Sawyer County Board of Supervisors voted 12 to three to "discontinue the practice of permitting private hunting cabins on county forest land." And they established the date to end the practice as no later than December 31, 2010.

There's probably no end to the list of good reasons why
that had to happen, but it changed the lives and traditions of a
lot of lives—at least the 100 cabin permit holders—including
my husband's "Blue Heaven" Camp 52, which has been nes-
tled in the Sawyer County Forest since 1952 when his father,
Marv Hanson, built it along with the other four original "Jolly
Boys:" Adder Madson, Merle Dunster, Kenneth Sugrue and
Howard Nystrom. Those Jolly Boys shared that part of the
county forest with other hunting camps now folding too—
Camp No Hunt, Camp Handicap, Dynamite Hill and Bare
Naked Purgatory Swamp—names steeped in shared history
and humor.

The night before John left for camp, the living room was
filled with his tightly packed army duffel bag, the familiar vin-
tage suitcase, the boxes of spirits and canned goods and the
leftover Halloween candy. When I came home from work at
5:30 p.m., I asked him if he didn't want to leave right then. The
preparations were so obviously ready that they called out to
me, "I can hardly wait to get there."

And I admit that every year I feel a jealous tug as that
camp—like nothing else in our life together—completely
takes over John's mind and psyche. He reminds me of my
younger brothers when I was a kid, and how they awaited
Christmas morning so they could open the gifts. It is sheer,
unbridled love of the deer camp.

So I was prepared this year to write this column in a hu-
morous vein, pointing out the childish ways and rigid traditions that occupy the minds of the same group of nine or ten
grown men who convene up there during what Hayward has
dubbed "holy week," a term that would offend all of the nuns
who so carefully provided me with a Roman Catholic ele-
mentary education in the lives and feasts of all the saints.

Alas, I can't summon up the humor I was so looking forward to sharing. It's gone. As will be the shack and the years and years and years of things done all over again the same way, decade after decade, for the sake and memory of the original Jolly Boys who founded Blue Heaven.

My husband left the house with a heavy heart that Friday morning before opening day. The week would be spent with all of the guys trying to sort out where to build the next shack, what to do with the old shack and its worthless but irreplaceable contents, how to disassemble a shack that holds the memories of births, marriages, grandchildren, deaths and beyond. A shack that one year, shortly after Marvin Hanson died, showed his visage at a window outside during a violent night storm.

As a point of clarification that may not be needed to this reading audience, the hunting camp is really not about the deer, although they are the *raison d'etre* for hunting camps like my husband's. It's about tradition. It's about passing the torch. It's about love.

So I will share only one piece of humor that originally was planned for this column. When John comes home for Thanksgiving and then leaves again very early the next morning—always a Friday, of course—he tiptoes up to the bedroom to say goodbye to me. He can't mask the eagerness and the excitement I see in him as he returns to the shack. Even on Thanksgiving Day, as he carves the turkey, his mind is at the shack. I can see it in his eyes and I can hear it in his head, even though he doesn't speak of it. He sits on the side of the bed and I pretend to wake up. He leans over, kisses me and says, "I'm going to mount up."

Yes, that is what he says. The allure and mystery and thrill of the hunt permeates even his language and he imagines himself, I suppose, getting back on his horse to go back into the woods. Year after year, he has said, "I'm going to mount up," and it wasn't until last year that I finally asked him if a horse had replaced his luxury van sitting in the driveway.

But this year was different. He didn't say he was going to mount up. His eyes didn't reflect back the thrill and excitement of the hunt. He seemed subdued, somehow resigned. And I felt his loss. Surely, his father Marvin is not happy about all of this. Nor are John's sons, or his cousin or his other hunting brothers. They are all wondering what happens now. How do we hang on to all those memories contained in the walls of this dilapidated, falling-down, asbestos-shingled camp that has raised us from childhood to boyhood into adulthood and beyond? Where do we go now? Will it ever be the same?

I have no answers, except to say, "mount up" you hunters, and carry those memories and traditions with you as you take your leave of Camp 52. Set up your new camp. Call it Blue Heaven. Make sure young John Dennis Hanson shoots his first buck from that camp, surrounded by all of you who will still be there. Light your fires, play your cards, tell your stories. And look for Marvin in the windows, because he'll be watching.

Deer season 2009 began like most of the deer seasons before it. I met Dennis at the area where we parked our vehicles on the Friday before season. The two of us unloaded the Coot from the trailer, loaded it with supplies, and began our trek toward the shack. Rob had hired a surveyor to mark off the boundaries of the southeast corner of the Club 27 property that we hoped to purchase, and the bright orange ribbons marking the property lines were visible as we started to trudge toward the shack. About midway down the well-worn logging road, we stopped the Coot

Dennis examines a clearing on the six acres sold to us by Club 27 where we decided to build New Blue.

and walked into the woods to see if we could locate the southeast corner stake. It wasn't difficult to find, and we were both very pleased to discover that the southeast corner was where we had thought it would be. It was on high ground, not in a swampy area as we had feared, and there was an excellent building site in a small open area surrounded by tall pine trees. We were eager to tell the others on their arrival.

The weather was balmy for November 20, 2009, and the road in to camp was relatively dry. Ollie, Billie-Bob, Mike, and Nate arrived a short time later, followed by Barry. Rob was still in Atlanta studying for a test for his master's degree and had to delay his arrival until Sunday. We unloaded and put away the supplies, and I prepared a large batch of church barbecues for our lunch. We spent the afternoon taking care of camp chores and putting up tree stands for opening day the next morning. Our usual poker game with the traditional snacks and beverages occurred on schedule by 5 p.m., followed by one of our traditional Reali spaghetti dinners. We cleaned the kitchen, turned the light plant off, and lit the candle. We all crawled into our bunks by 11 p.m. to rest up for the big opener.

As I settled into my bunk that had been occupied by my father for so many years, I once again began to soak up all the sounds of the shack that had become so very familiar to me. The antique shack clock was tick-tick-ticking, waiting to sound its loud, obnoxious alarm in the early morning hours. The fire in our old wood cookstove was crackling and still producing ample heat to make the water kettles hiss a little steam. Several of my fellow hunters had already drifted off into slumber, and a serenade of snoring came from various parts of the bunk area. It was a peaceful, relaxing, and familiar atmosphere, and I couldn't believe that all of it was coming to an end. I eventually drifted off to sleep with my senses still absorbing everything that was so important to me about that hunting camp.

At 5 a.m., the antique alarm clock went off. The clock never just rang; there would always be several short dings before it got into full ringing mode. This was a good thing, as it prepared us for what was to come a few seconds later. As usual, none of us wanted to crawl out of our warm, comfortable bunks, but we all began to stir. We each needed to prepare before we set off into the woods to begin the hunt. It was twenty-five degrees, and the forecast called for a high around fifty degrees that day.

My cousin, Billie-Bob, shot his first buck, a small deer with spike antlers, in the Little Rocks area. He rushed back to camp to claim the buck money that was attached to the shack wall with an icepick. Dennis slew a spike buck on the Upper Swamp Road shortly thereafter, and Nate downed a six-pointer about 10:30 a.m. Three bucks hung from the buck pole. We celebrated our success with Bloody Marys, followed by venison breakfast

My sons, Rob and Ollie, with me standing between them

sausage Billie-Bob had made from last season's deer kill, along with pancakes and fried eggs. Several of us saw deer during the afternoon hunt, but no one had a chance for a kill shot. That evening we roasted a fourteen-pound prime-rib roast to medium-rare perfection in the old woodstove and complemented it with garlic mashed potatoes and Caesar salad.

My son Robin arrived from Atlanta at 6 a.m. on Sunday and departed immediately for the Big Rock, where I had seen three deer on opening morning. Ollie shot a doe up by the Can that morning, but the deer hunting was difficult, as there was no snow in the woods. By the end of the day, we had four deer hanging and were pleased with the results of our hunt thus far.

The remainder of deer season 2009 progressed as usual, with all the good food, the fun poker games, and hunters coming and going throughout the season. After brunch on Monday, Dennis, Rob, Ollie, and I kicked everyone else out of the shack so we could sit down to have a serious discussion about the future of the camp. Although we discussed the possibility of hunting from our current location during deer season 2010, we all knew that that would be unrealistic because it would leave us with only a month to vacate after the season ended. If the weather wasn't cooperating, we would be hard-pressed to accomplish everything that needed to be done. We decided that this season would be the last season at the current location. Dennis and I also decided that day to bequeath all of the camp assets to Rob, who was then forty-two, and Ollie, who was thirty-seven. They would become equal partners and the new owners of Blue Heaven. Dennis and I would take on the role of advisors, but my two sons would be in charge from that point forth. Meanwhile, Rob would work on concluding a deal with Club 27 to purchase six acres in the southeast corner of their property so we could begin the disassembly and moving of the shack to the new location.

On the final Sunday of the season, we awoke to snow on the ground, too late to do us much good, as it was time to pack up and leave. Breakfast was prepared, and everyone seemed somber knowing that this day might be the last one any of us would spend in this hunting camp that had endured since 1955. While we ate our final meal at the shack, there was much talk of the Jolly Boys of old who would always have one final game of poker before breaking camp on Sunday afternoon, then congregate with their wives at Gerlach's Landing on Nelson Lake later for burgers and tap beer. It was an era filled with great memories.

BLOODY MARYS

Bloody Marys have been a staple at our hunting camp for as long as I can remember. We simply call them "Bloodies" and they are never served until late morning during deer camp just prior to our large brunch at noon. As tradition has it, we don't allow Bloodies to be served until there is meat hanging from the deer pole. This provides incentive for everyone on the first day of deer season to shoot a deer and get it hanging back at camp before noon so we don't wind up without a Bloody to celebrate the hunt.

I've tasted numerous recipes for Bloody Marys and most are far too spicy for me to enjoy. We make ours slightly on the mild side, and anyone that enjoys a Bloody with a kick can certainly add Tabasco sauce, cayenne pepper, or horseradish to their drink if they find it too mild. I give the credit for this recipe to Russ Clagett, who co-owned and operated Herman's Landing for more than twenty-five years and was known for his prowess in putting together a tasty Bloody Mary. As Russ said, "Start with your smallest ingredient and work your way up when making a mixed drink." It works.

Preparation

Use a sizable glass for the Bloody. Something in the 12- to 18-ounce area works best. Fill the glass about two-thirds full of ice. Add celery salt on top of the ice, shaking the container about six to eight times. Next, add four or five large squirts of Worcestershire sauce. Add an ounce and a half of your favorite vodka and the juice of a large wedge of lemon that has been squeezed to get as much lemon juice into the drink as possible. Finally, fill the glass with a combination of 50 percent V8 juice and 50 percent Clamato Juice. Salt and pepper is optional, but not really needed. Use a fork to stir thoroughly. Garnish with a beef or celery stick, kosher pickle spear, olives, or whatever you feel is appropriate. Wasn't that easy? Serve with a "snit" of your favorite ice-cold beer. Put out the Tabasco, horseradish, and other spices for those who want to burn their lips.

Each Bloody Mary glass has a hunter's name on it and contains a venison stick to stir the ingredients.

From Old to New

We received Club 27's permission to begin work on the new site in the summer of 2010. To ease the transition, Dennis came up with the idea of calling Blue Heaven "Old Blue." So the new camp was named "New Blue."

During the winter of 2009–2010, Dennis and I attended multiple meetings with the Town of Lenroot and Sawyer County Zoning to obtain approval for a Special Use Permit to relocate the camp. On the last weekend of April 2010, Dennis, Ollie, Billie-Bob, Mike, and Brian Lane went to Old Blue for cleanup and disassembly. Rob was in Atlanta working, while Barry was at home recovering from knee surgery. I was out of town that weekend with my wife. The road into camp was bone-dry due to a drought, so transportation was not a problem. Ollie built a burn barrel out of an old garbage can, and they began to burn a lot of the junk that had accumulated in the camp over the past fifty-five years. They cleaned out the shanty, and boxed up items that would be needed at the new location, including dishes and cooking utensils.

The Playboy centerfolds that had served as decoration in the rafters of the shack for so many years were carefully removed and packed away for safekeeping and possible use at New Blue. Although we had heard rumors that the Sawyer County Board might be considering extending the Recreational Use Permits, we weren't optimistic that that would become a reality, so we proceeded with our plan to relocate. We made it our goal to ready the New Blue site and make it habitable by deer season 2010.

Late August gave us a clear and sunny day with temperatures in the low eighties, and abundant mosquitoes and deer flies. We met with Danny Thompson and his brother Mark, of Thompson Sand & Gravel, to lay out and dig footings for New Blue. We decided on the site for the new shack. We then used the eighteen-inch auger attached to Danny's crawler to dig fifteen four-foot holes for the Sonotubes. Danny also brought his Bobcat to haul in gravel and a pallet of concrete to fill the Sonotubes at a later date.

On September 5, 2010, we received word that the last of the original Jolly Boys, Merle Dunster, had passed away at the Hayward Hospital Nursing Home. The attendance at his funeral was huge, and his attachment to the hunting camp was evident in the photo boards displayed in the narthex of the church. Those in attendance exchanged many fond memories of this icon of Hayward. Merle, along with my father and Adder, had always been the stabilizing force of our hunting camp, and the void that his passing left simply emphasized all of the changes occurring as we moved forward to rebuild the camp at the new location.

In mid-September we poured concrete into the fifteen Sonotubes to serve as support pillars for New Blue. The weather was great, with clear skies and temperatures in the low sixties. We constructed a large box of treated wood that would be placed in a hole in the ground for the new privy to sit on. The next day we poured a concrete slab for the new light plant building. We waited a week for the concrete to set and then returned on Friday, September 24, 2010, to haul in lumber for the floor joists and new deck for New Blue. Hauling in the building supplies proved difficult. It had rained more than two inches, and the road was a mess. We built a makeshift road through the woods to the new site that quickly turned to a sea of mud with deep ruts and holes,

All lumber from Old Blue is salvaged for use in the reconstruction of New Blue. The asbestos siding and rotten floor joists and shingles were taken to a proper disposal site.

but we were able to wiggle our way in with the aide of winches on the vehicles. We installed the subfloor that day and then tarped everything to keep the floor from warping in the rain. That evening we returned to Old Blue to spend one last night there before the disassembly process began.

Our last night in Old Blue was memorable. I think that the excitement and anticipation of a new and improved hunting camp negated much of the disappointment we had been feeling, and we awoke Saturday morning to clear skies and a beautiful fall day. We ate a quick breakfast. Then Dennis, Robin, Ollie, Barry, Brian, and Michael went to the New Blue site to finish building a new woodshed, haul the outhouse to the new site, and put up a new buck pole. I stayed behind at Old Blue to empty the cupboards and pack up all of the remaining contents. Our work party agreed to return on October 8 and 9 to finish the disassembly.

Ollie and Mike Schaaf cut the walls of Old Blue into eight-foot sections, to be transported via trailer and reassembled at New Blue.

By early October, we had finally obtained our building permit, and the big weekend arrived with leafless trees and beautiful weather. The roof was peeled off, and we loaded the unsalvageable debris into a trailer to be hauled to a demolition site. We made numerous trips to the dump to dispose of all the debris and old mattresses. We also discarded the old wood-burning stove. It had served its purpose and was almost burned out. As we disassembled the shack, we were shocked at the number of mice nests hidden inside and the number of wolf spiders that were making their home within the building. Wolf spiders are huge and resemble tarantulas. They scattered, trying to find new shelter as the shack came tumbling down around them. By day's end, Camp 52 was completely disassembled, except for the shanty and shack floor. Naturally, everyone was exhausted from a day of back-breaking work and ready to head into town for a good night's rest.

On Saturday morning, the entire crew was on-site early. We transported the walls of Old Blue to the new site and installed

Ollie and Mike ensure that the old walls are plumb before nailing them into place on the subfloor of New Blue.

them atop the new subfloor. We were meticulous. We made certain that everything was square and level in the reconstruction process and installed the roof trusses and OSB board that afternoon. We ended the day by tarping the roof and temporarily attaching plywood over the window and door openings after hauling the majority of the interior contents to the new building. By 7 p.m. everyone was exhausted and sore but pleased about what had been accomplished. New Blue was rapidly taking shape.

Over the course of the next several weekends, anyone who could make himself available was at New Blue frantically working to get things put back together in anticipation of deer season 2010. Shingles were put on the roof, soffits were installed, electrical wires were run for the lighting, and the boot racks were reinstalled, as was the old oil burner and an updated wood-burning cookstove. The stovepipes were reconnected, and a new asbestos chimney was put in place. We lit the first fires to warm New Blue on October 29, 2010. We reinstalled the kitchen counter and sink and reconnected the plumbing. The shelving unit was rehung so we could unload the boxes of dishes and make them accessible. The new shanty was on deadline, so we had an area for storage, but the light plant had to be reinstalled and fired up so we could have light at night.

The Old Blue site had to be completely cleaned up and void of any debris for inspection by the county in order for us to receive the full refund of several thousand dollars that the county was holding for removal charges in the event they were needed. A portion of our lease payment had been placed in a trust fund each year in the event that we abandoned the building and the county had to remove the camp from Sawyer County forestland when our lease terminated. As we worked on both sites, there were many evenings when several of us simply camped out on the unfinished floor of New Blue. The new bunk area wouldn't be completed until November 5, 2010, when we took delivery of nine new designer mattresses.

On Sunday, November 7, 2010, the demolition work and removal of debris from Old Blue was completed and Old Blue was no more. By November 13, there was already half a foot of snow on the ground, and we were relieved that we had completed our mission of moving and reconstructing the shack with only days to spare before the weather would have made things impossible.

There were still many projects left to be done, but we were all confident that many could be completed during deer season 2010, which was scheduled to start on November 20. Except for being four feet wider, the interior of New Blue looked exactly like Old Blue. We were amazed at what we had accomplished in such a short period of time and looked forward to hunting out of this renovated hunting camp in a couple of weeks.

New Blue,
2010–2011

All the regular hunters at Blue Heaven who were available spent every weekend in the fall of 2010 frantically working to prepare the new hunting camp for the upcoming deer season. One of the priority projects was to complete the framework for the new bunks so we could take delivery of the nine new designer mattresses Rob had ordered to replace the fifty-five-year-old mattresses that we had thrown out when dismantling Old Blue. The new mattresses were very thick and firm. They would be a huge improvement over the swayback mattresses and old-fashioned springs on which we had slept for so many years. It took us only a day to complete the project, and every hunter looked forward to organizing his assigned bunk area in time for deer season.

We agreed that deer season 2010 would be a combined deer hunt and work party to finish off the interior of New Blue, as there was still considerable interior finishing to be accomplished. The ceiling and walls were as yet unfinished, and the flooring still needed to be applied. We would use the salvaged lumber from Old Blue to complete these tasks and would also apply the old tongue-and-groove maple flooring from Old Blue over the OSB subflooring. Our goal was to recycle and use as much of the lumber from Old Blue as possible in finishing off the interior, not only to save on the cost of construction but also to retain the history and ambience of Old Blue. New Blue also required additional weatherproofing, as numerous areas still needed caulk and sealing to help retain heat within the building during the cold nights of deer season. We decided that we would spend the first weekend of deer season hunting, hoping to get some venison hanging on the new buck pole. We would then devote the majority of the rest of the season to working on the various construction projects.

In mid-November, we arrived at New Blue for the hunt. Everyone was thrilled to see the results of our hard labor over the previous summer and fall. We celebrated with a champagne-and-prime-rib dinner on the opening Saturday evening of deer camp, toasting each other for all of the hard work and sacrifices we each had made to provide us with a new hunting camp.

Although the temperatures only reached the midteens during the day and there was snow on the ground, we felt relatively comfortable in our new surroundings. We were fortunate to harvest five deer that season and considered it a success. We spent many days at camp unpacking boxes of dishes and other items that had been moved to New Blue from Old Blue late in the fall. Ollie located an old-fashioned Schlitz beer sign and had it cleaned up

A new sign for New Blue

Ollie and Mike attach rough-sawn pine planks for exterior siding while Brian Hanson and Brian Lane apply roofing paper as an underlayment.

with new lettering. He wired its lights to the light plant and installed it on the new buck pole. We also returned to the site of Old Blue, as there was enough snow on the ground to burn the remaining pile of scrap lumber unfit for use at New Blue. The former site of Blue Heaven had now been totally cleared and soon would be reclaimed by the forest.

After we closed up New Blue at the end of deer season 2010, the camp sat idle through the winter. We returned in the first weekend in April 2011 to find that it had wintered without any problems. Although the temperature was in the midfifties, there was still a half foot of snow on the ground. However, that did not deter us from the many projects we wanted to accomplish. We sealed up areas on the roof overhangs attractive to critters and bugs, cut up and split additional wood for the wood-burning stove, and tackled numerous other small projects in preparation for closing up the camp for the summer months. We doubted that any of us would return during the summer, as there simply were too many mosquitoes, deer flies, and other bugs to make visiting New Blue a pleasurable experience. We also made plans to build a bridge across a portion of the swamp leading from our parking area into New Blue, as often the swamp was too wet to make maneuvering across it an easy journey. There was much discussion about what needed to be done when we returned in the fall. A priority item was to construct a new light plant building to enclose the light plant that was sitting out in the elements covered by a tarp when not in use.

When we returned that fall, we came loaded with a new, prebuilt light plant building, used metal dock sections for the new bridge, and the necessary tools to begin the task of putting down the wood floor and installing wood paneling inside New Blue. Ollie had also located a Jewel wood-burning cookstove. Much was accomplished that weekend. We installed the light plant building atop its concrete pad, and the new cookstove. Ollie brought his planer along, and several of us ran all the wood from Old Blue through the planer to clean it up for reinstallation in New Blue. By the weekend's end, the maple flooring had been installed, and much of the interior paneling was also adorning the walls. We no longer thought of New Blue as a hunting "shack." It was quickly being transformed into a hunting "lodge"! All of us were now confident that we had accomplished our goal in moving and rebuilding Blue Heaven. We would keep the dream of the Jolly Boys alive not only for us, but also for those who would follow in the Jolly Boys' footsteps in the years to come. We all looked forward to making new memories in New Blue.

Shack Rules

From the outset, the Jolly Boys believed that certain rules of conduct had to be established to assure harmony within their hunting camp. The rules would apply to all, with no exceptions. They thought that these rules would be instrumental in helping their camp succeed, as all knew that a great deal of effort would be needed to have up to nine hunters living together for up to nine days during the Wisconsin deer hunt. The rules addressed hygiene and behavior, as well as other commonsense concerns, and increased in scope as the years went by. If you are planning a new hunting camp of your own or are already involved in an established hunting camp, rule number one is to not forget the rules. Rule number two is to always remember rule number one.

1. No one is allowed to return from the facilities provided outside to relieve themselves without washing their hands immediately on their return. There are never any exceptions to this hygiene rule and it will be carefully monitored.

2. There will be no teeth brushing or dental flossing allowed inside the shack. This is to be done outside as there is to be no spitting in the sink area or near counters that we are using for the preparation of food and for dishwashing.

3. No hats are allowed to be worn at the table when eating breakfast, lunch, or dinner, or while playing cards. ~~No elbows are allowed on the table while dining. Bad~~ manners while dining will not be tolerated.

4. No licking of knives is allowed. Anyone caught licking their knife and attempting to use it to take butter from the butter dish will have their hand severed at the wrist.

5. Any hunter that damages camp property will be required to replace that property at his own expense.

6. All poker games are limited to nickel/dime bets per preestablished shack betting rules. The maximum anyone is allowed to lose or win on any given hand on progressive card games is limited to two dollars. Stakes for cribbage games are twenty-five cents per game with fifty cents for a skunk unless the players agree beforehand to larger stakes.

7. Preestablished shack rules apply to all card games. If a dispute arises and the shack rules don't address the situation, The Book of Hoyle will be consulted.

8. No one is allowed to leave their clothing or personal gear on chairs and in other areas of the shack. All personal belongings have to be stowed at all times in the designated individual locker areas. Any excess clothing and gear is to be stowed in sealed plastic bins and left in the shelter of the outside wood shed.

9. Boots and shoes not being worn are to be hung in the ceiling boot rack. Boots, shoes, and socks are not to be left unattended on the floor.

10. No one is allowed to invite a guest up to camp without the express consent of all Jolly Boys. There are no exceptions and any guest must have the preapproval of everyone at camp.

11. Everyone is required to take their turn at doing dishes and other kitchen chores. This rule does not apply to the individual who has cooked the meal.

12. Everyone is expected to share in the chores of bringing in wood, sweeping the floor, and keeping the interior of the shack clean with everything in its proper place.

13. No loaded firearms are allowed inside the shack. Rifles are to be kept in the outside enclosed gun rack for everyone's safety. If a rifle becomes jammed or wet from the weather and it is necessary to bring the weapon in for maintenance, it will be done under the supervision of the Jolly Boys and inspected to be certain it is unloaded prior to bringing it into the shack.

14. For the safety of everyone, all hunters hunting out of the hunting camp have to be at least fourteen years of age before they are permitted to hunt with a rifle by themselves. It is permissible for a twelve-year-old to hunt with a rifle if he's had a hunter safety course and hunts within sight of his father.

15. All tools and camp maintenance equipment are to be neatly stored in the attached shanty in their designated areas at all times.

16. The bunk area is to be kept as cool and smoke-free as possible and it is the responsibility of all to keep the curtains to that area drawn.

17. Any hunter or camp guest that has any issues with the shack rules is welcome to find a different hunting camp in which to hunt.

18. It is the obligation of any hunter who receives permission to invite a guest to the hunting shack to familiarize the guest with the shack rules and to assist in enforcing the rules.

Conclusion

By the fall of 2011, a stranger could walk by the former site of Camp 52 on the old fading logging road and wouldn't suspect that a hunting camp had been situated on Sawyer County forestlands at this location for fifty-five years. All the debris is gone and nature has reclaimed the site. There is no evidence left to indicate that this was once the home of the hunting camp known as Blue Heaven, occupied by a group of men for at least nine days out of the year who called themselves the Jolly Boys. If one continued to walk down this old logging road for about a quarter mile to the east, they would come across a relatively new hunting camp with a Schlitz beer sign hanging by the buck pole with the name Blue Heaven on it. If they entered the hunting camp now known as New Blue, they would find an almost exact replica of the old hunting shack. All of the furnishings on the interior were salvaged and remain the same. The pots, pans, and dishes are the same. The walls, windows, doors, and flooring are all the same, and the interior design of the camp remains the same. Any one of the Jolly Boys of old could walk through the door of the new hunting shack and swear that he was in the Blue Heaven of old. He would find the same traditions, the same rules, the same menu items being prepared on and in a similar wood-burning cookstove. He would hear the same old stories that have been told time and time again.

Except for the new cookstove and a new sink countertop, the kitchen area of
New Blue is an exact replica of the kitchen in Old Blue.

Everything would be completely familiar to him. He would be
proud that the Jolly Boys' legacy continues.

This is the end of my story, but it's not the end of our story.
My hope is that it's just the beginning. My dream is that the traditions of the Jolly Boys and their hunting camp will continue
on through the generations for my sons, their children, and their
grandchildren.

Acknowledgments

If you spent the many hours necessary to read through all the entries in the three shack logs, you would see why Blue Heaven was beloved by so many in the Hayward and Cable area. More than two hundred people have graced the interior of that little hunting shack that was situated on county forestland over the course of five decades.

The five original Jolly Boys of Marvin, Merle, Adder, Howard, and Ken extended invitations to Clifford Bergum, Dennis and Russ Clagett, John Dunster, Brian Hanson, John Hanson, Bobby Hanson, Rob Hanson, Ollie Hanson, Sam Helms, Bob Larson, Peter and Philip Madson, Dale Nystrom, and Norm Schmickel to join them in the hunt over the course of three decades. Second-generation owners John Hanson and Dennis Clagett extended invitations to Brian and Blade Lane, Phillip Rasmussen, Barry Rice, Lester and Michael Schaaf, Nate Schmitz, Dennis Skare, and several others to partake in the hunt as room in the hunting camp allowed. Third-generation owners Rob and Ollie Hanson continue that tradition by inviting others to hunt with us, and the spouses of many of these hunters have also been invited to share in the experience of the hunting shack when deer season wasn't in progress.

In addition to those who hunted with the Jolly Boys during deer season, a multitude of people paid a visit to the hunting shack by invitation when deer season wasn't in progress. The shack log reflects most of the Jolly Boys' visitors and they included Lester and Helen Anderson, Inard "I.O." and Adah Anderson, Bobby Anderson, Tom and Betty Beckwith, Carl Benson, Romaine Berg, Clifford and Ruby Bergum with their sons Bobby and Richard, Harold and Lois Cadott, Bob and Karen Churitch, Nate DeLong, Milt and Alice Dieckman, Tom Duffy, Robert and Georgia Dunster, Chester and Edith Erickson, Harry Erickson, Hank and Toots Erickson, Adrian and Flowell Faase, Dick Gillis, Don and Elaine Gillis, Ed Gobler, Harold Gobler, Henry Gunderson, Tom and Isla Hamms, Ken and Carol Hanson, Father Bob Hanson, Arnold Hanson, Cliff Hanson, Porky Hanson, Sammy and Kathy Helms, Vern and Betty Inhoff, Clarence "Punce" Johnson, Curt Karbalis, Jim and Mary Kirby, Art Klett, Stan Knutson, Ray and Ann Lajmel, Robin Larson, Stan and Goody Laska, Wes Lindahl, Bob and Carol Longtine, Pastor Jim Mangulsen, Dennis and Delores Marquart, Metro and Mary Maznio, Scott and Connie Miller, Jack and Colleen Moreland, Dane Nelson, Carl Nordquist, Norm and Charlotte Reisterer, Hank and Gert Rieckhoff, Walter Risberg, Art and Doris Rude, Emil and Theresa Rude, Dr. Sahs, Gordy and Jeane Ann Skamser, Harold Tiffany, Dennis and Marlene Trembley, Dick Walker, Michael Wetter, Blaine and Mary Wickland, Lyman and Edna Williamson, Ward and Linda Williamson, and Dr. Don and Margaret Willison as well as many, many others who didn't sign in to the official shack log. Many of these former guests are now departed, but all have left their memories imbedded in those of us who remain.

This book wouldn't have been possible without the encouragement and skillful editing of my wife, Kathryn Mortwedt-Hanson; my sister-in-law, Dianne Mortwedt-Kramer; and Dianne's close friend and accomplished editor, Mary Rogers. These ladies were all instrumental in making the story more readable and engaging. Special thanks to those women whose lives have been all about reading and writing.

About the Author

John Marvin Hanson was born and raised in Hayward, Wisconsin. After spending a career in the insurance industry, he and his wife, Kathryn, are semi-retired and spend the majority of their time at their lake home near Hayward.